REAL· _BS

MIDLANDS

Pub Interiors of Special Historic Interest

Edited by **Paul Ainsworth**

Best wishes
Paul Ainsworth

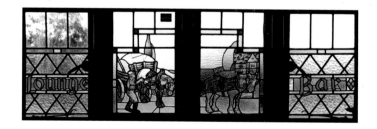

CAMPAIGN
FOR
REAL ALE

Based on CAMRA's East and West Midlands Regional Inventories of Historic Pub Interiors

Produced by CAMRA's Pub Heritage Group
www.heritagepubs.org.uk
info.pubheritage@camra.org.uk

Published by the Campaign for Real Ale Ltd
230 Hatfield Road, St Albans,
Hertfordshire AL1 4LW
www.camra.org.uk/books

© Campaign for Real Ale 2015

First published 2015

ISBN 978-1-85249-324-0

A CIP catalogue record for this book is available from the
British Library

Printed and bound in Malta by Latitude Press Ltd

Head of Publishing: Simon Hall
Project Editor: Julie Hudson
Series designer & consultant: Dale Tomlinson
Title designer: Andy Shaw
Maps: Mark Walker, WildPixel Ltd
Sales & Marketing: David Birkett

Photo credits
Photographs © Michael
Slaughter LRPS, apart from the
following;
(Key: t=top, b=bottom,
m=middle, l=left, r=right)
Page 20 (ml) by Laurie Wilson
Page 36 by Alan Cooke
Page 37 by Alan Cooke
Page 38 by Alan Cooke
Page 87 by Geoff Brandwood
Page 92 (br) by Geoff Brandwood
Page 95 by Geoff Brandwood
Page 97 (tl) by Geoff Brandwood
Page 101 by Geoff Brandwood
Page 110 by Geoff Brandwood

Cover and title pictures
Front cover: the main lobby at the
Bartons Arms, Aston,
Birmingham, 1900-1, with its
sumptuous Minton tiling and
rare snob screens

Back cover: The Coopers Tavern,
Burton-on-Trent, is one of very
few pubs to have no conventional
bar counter

Page 1 (title page): Lounge bar
windows at the Waggon &
Horses, South Reston,
Lincolnshire, 1930s

Page 2 (this page): tile paintings
at the Fighting Cocks, Moseley,
Birmingham, by Craven Dunnill
of Jackfield, 1898-9

Editor's Acknowldegements
Please see page 123

Contents

Pubs to Cherish

Real Heritage Pubs of the Midlands celebrates the 201 pub interiors in the region which CAMRA has identified as having special historic interest. They represent an important aspect of the area's cultural and built heritage and several are treasures of national stature.

That said, they account for only 2% or so of all the pubs in the Midlands – why is that so? A major reason, of course, is that pub interiors have always been subject to change. The only pubs which are exactly the same as the day they opened are ones which came into being in the last few years. The pace of change, though, has accelerated. Most of our remaining historic pubs evolved slowly over time and clung on to their more endearing features. Recent times unfortunately have seen a mania for opening out, faddish theming, image change and general trashing. Consequently, many a pub has suffered regular makeovers during which most, if not all, vestiges of original or early features have been lost.

The irony here is that interest in historic buildings has never been greater. Lots of us are fascinated by our built heritage and spend many an hour visiting old properties from stately homes to the most vernacular of structures. This broadening of interest is reflected in National Trust openings like the Birmingham Back-to-Backs and Mr Straw's House, Worksop. All the sadder, then, that genuine pub interiors seem so under-valued by mainstream conservationists and that owners are often eager to tear them apart.

It is CAMRA that has picked up the baton on behalf of our pub heritage, filling the gaps in knowledge of what is out there and actively seeking to protect what is left. This is the seventh in a series of regional guides to our best heritage pubs and draws on many years of work by CAMRA members to track down and record those interiors which have escaped the attention of the modernisers and 'improvers'. Many also serve great traditional real ale but all offer much else for you to enjoy.

The Olde Trip to Jerusalem cuts into the rock under Nottingham Castle. This is Mortimer's Room, fitted out around 1930

What Shaped Pubs in the Midlands?

Is there such a thing as a 'typical' Midlands pub? Given that the Midlands covers such a large and varied area and that the region's pubs have taken shape over many years, the answer is a resounding 'no'. By and large, pubs developed in much the same ways as in the rest of the country. Nonetheless, as we shall see, examples of distinctive local designs and layouts survive in some towns and cities, the result generally of particular brewers evolving their own house styles. But first, a bit of history.

In the Beginning

Most early public houses were literally just that – ordinary houses whose owners decided to open up a room or two to sell drink to neighbours. Pub keeping was a family business and, especially in the countryside, usually part-time. All you needed was somewhere to store the merchandise, someone to serve it and somewhere for customers to drink it. Nearly all these very homely pubs have gone now but the Midlands has perhaps the best surviving example – the Sun, Leintwardine, Herefordshire (p.32), which, until recently, had just a basic single public room with drinks fetched from the kitchen. Remarkably, this arrangement is preserved, albeit within the now-expanded pub.

An even simpler layout can be found at the Cider House, Defford, Worcestershire (p.109) (one of just four cider-only houses in the country) where, in good weather, the garden is the main bar, with service from a hatch.

The other kinds of establishment up until the early 19th century were the tavern and the inn. The former existed only in larger towns, catering for the more prosperous customer by serving wine and food. They were never common and no former

Sun, Leintwardine, Herefordshire: the simply-appointed 'Brick Bar' is typical of how rooms in thousands of country pubs must once have appeared. It is an extraordinarily rare survival

taverns survive in the Midlands. Inns provided meals and accommodation for the better-off traveller along with stabling for their horses. Two Lincolnshire pubs, the Angel & Royal, Grantham, and George, Stamford, are old inns though both have been refitted in modern times.

The Golden Age

The pub as we know it is mostly a Victorian creation. The first part of the 19th century saw the widespread adoption of counter service and the hand-pumped beer engine, heralding the change from an essentially domestic environment to a form of shop which could handle a greater volume of trade. This was overlain with the complexities of Victorian societal structure, hence compartmentalised interiors whose different grades of room reflected the many social distinctions which existed, even among working people. Later in the century, under the influence of social reformers and the powerful Temperance lobby, a drive to improve public houses took hold. This enhanced the multi-room principle with its ability to offer a choice of 'better' rooms and thus attract a respectable clientele.

The years around 1900 proved to be the high point of pub-building and design, with grand, ornate 'palace' pubs arriving in the bigger towns and cities, but also with lesser variants being built elsewhere. Birmingham is blessed with one of the most spectacular products of this era – the Bartons Arms, Aston (p.83).

On a more modest scale but still richly rewarding are the likes of the Anchor (p.85), White Swan (p.88) and Woodman (p.89) all in Birmingham's Digbeth area. The building of such pubs can be linked to an assertive 'fewer but better' policy on the part of Birmingham's magistrates (see p.86)

Of course, most Victorian pubs remained small, local affairs. The 1830 Beer Act made it much easier and cheaper to open a pub, hence

In total contrast to the Sun (opposite) the Bartons Arms, Aston, is the most lavish Victorian pub surviving in Birmingham and symbolises the great age of pub-building around 1900

Lounge at the Vine, Stoke-on-Trent

the ensuing explosion in numbers – over 33,000 new ones in the next two years. These beerhouses (they couldn't sell wine or spirits) were generally the simple successor to the alehouse and most have vanished. As the century wore on, these local pubs became larger and less plain but without pretence of catering for other than the working chap. Pubs like the Vine, Stoke-on-Trent (p.78), and the Duke of York, Elton, Derbyshire (p.20), give a strong flavour of how such places looked and felt.

Between the Wars

During Edwardian times the pub-building spree tailed off and the Great War brought it to a full stop. After the war, pubs at first continued to be built on traditional lines, albeit with contemporary detailing. The Rose Villa Tavern of 1919-20 (p.91) in Birmingham's Jewellery Quarter, for instance, is a stripped-down version by architects Wood & Kendrick of the tile and terracotta pubs they had been building around 1900; it even has extensive wall-tiling very much in the Victorian mould. In the same city, the Villa Tavern, Nechells (p.93), of 1924-5 is in plain brick but the three separate rooms hark back to pre-war days and would be very familiar to Victorian drinkers, albeit with reduced decoration. At the Vine in Wednesfield (p.104), we find a no-nonsense working man's pub rebuilt in 1938 with detailing redolent of its times but a still deeply traditional three-room layout.

The inter-war years are best known, though, for the large-scale 'improved' pubs built for growing suburbs and main highways. Reducing the number of pubs but improving standards in what remained had been the mission of magistrates for some years and continued the objectives of the Victorian reformers. However, the 'fewer but better' slogan coined by Birmingham's magistrates now took on added significance with a concerted drive to broaden the appeal of pubs and reduce their dependence on alcohol sales alone. In contrast to being the haunt of 'disreputable' working-class drinkers, the idea was for pubs to offer a respectable environment whose range of rooms and facilities encouraged civilised behaviour and patronage by the middle-classes. And not only men, but women too (albeit in male company). Bigger pubs might also provide a home for outdoor bowling clubs, or a children's playground to encourage family visits.

Architectural Styles Between the Wars

Brewers responded with a fresh surge of pub-building from the mid-1920s, whilst also remodelling many smaller existing houses – the Olde Dolphin Inne, Derby exemplifying how old pubs could be given a new (in this case, ye olde) look.

Within this environment, it is not surprising that much pub-building had some architectural ambition. Perhaps the most emblematic inter-war architectural style was Art Deco but this was only rarely adopted for pubs. It was maybe thought that typical drinkers wanted something more traditional and homely. However, two Nottinghamshire hotels, the Vale, Arnold (p.52) and Test Match, West Bridgford (p.62) are splendid surviving examples of this sleek and elegant genre.

Many of the new pubs sported a restrained 17th century or neo-Georgian appearance, such as the British Oak, Stirchley, Birmingham of 1923-4 (p.94) and the Crystal Fountain, Cannock, Staffordshire of 1937 (p.72). Some of these were truly vast, a magnificent, intact example being the sprawling Berkeley, Scunthorpe, opened in 1940 (p.46).

The Berkeley, Scunthorpe, Lincolnshire, is a remarkably intact example of the great roadhouses that were built between the wars, offering many spacious rooms and a wide range of facilities. It opened in 1940.

Black Horse, Northfield, Birmingham, 'Brewers' Tudor', 1929

Rather more exciting was a Tudor-style evocation of an imagined Merrie England nicknamed 'Brewers' Tudor' for its extensive use of half-timbering. The most impressive Midlands example (if not in the whole country) is the Black Horse, Northfield, Birmingham (p.94), constructed in 1929 on a massive scale to resemble a half-timbered manor house and with suitably baronial trappings inside, some of which remain. In the same fashion, but much smaller, the Butchers Arms, Audley, Staffs (p.70) has much period-style detail within its brick and half-timbered exterior. A further good example is the Five Ways, Sherwood, Nottingham of 1936-7 (p.58).

Post-War Decline

Intact post-war pubs are very rare. This is the Punch Bowl, Worcester of 1958

After the Second World War, Britain was bankrupt and hardly any pubs were built for a decade. The new pubs that began emerging in the mid-1950s were typified, not surprisingly for these straightened times, by utilitarian design and use of low-quality materials. Layouts, though, still provided a choice of rooms and such customary features as off-sales and concert rooms. Needless to say, once the economy picked up, these cut-price reminders of the grey post-war years became highly unfashionable. Very, very few intact interiors of this period therefore remain but the Midlands has one of the best examples in the Punch Bowl, Worcester of 1958 (p.114). Although some may find it difficult to love, it's as precious in its own way as the Sun at Leintwardine.

The increased prosperity in the mid-1960s heralded a time of rapid and mostly regrettable change. The social divisions mirrored by the multi-roomed pub were vanishing whilst magistrates and police favoured direct supervision of all parts of a pub from the serving area – hence the widespread removal of internal walls to the great detriment of the atmosphere and attractiveness of most traditional pubs. At the same time, a series of brewery mergers brought the majority of pubs into the ownership of one or other of the 'Big Six' national brewing conglomerates. All of these, in thrall to their corporate accountants and marketing men, inflicted huge damage on the pub heritage they inherited. Smaller brewers and many private owners too shared this obsession to modernise.

And still it went on. The rise of off-licence shops and supermarkets made off-sales departments in pubs redundant. Environmental health officers demanded changes to accommodate inside toilets and better food preparation facilities. Old bar-back fittings were hacked about to make space for more varied products – wines, spirits, refrigerated drinks. Fire officers insisted on adaptations to provide safer escape routes. These relentless pressures resulted in a much-depleted pub heritage.

The Aftermath

Front bar, Test Match, West Bridgford, Nottinghamshire (Winner of a Pub Design Award, and also a 'Two Star' listed pub)

Recent years have seen a tragic decline in the overall number of traditional pubs in this country – down from around 70,000 to less than 50,000 since 1980. To some extent, this has been offset by the increase in bars, nearly all in town and city centres but, with some honourable exceptions, few of these have much merit in design terms and most will no doubt undergo a complete makeover every few years. New pubs are still being built though conversions from other buildings like banks and shops are much more common. It's noteworthy that in most years no winner can be found for the New Build category in CAMRA's annual Pub Design Awards – and also that at least two previous winners have subsequently been trashed and remodelled.

On the other hand, public interest in our built heritage has never been higher, as evidenced by the numbers of people visiting National Trust and English Heritage properties. The existence of this very book and the popularity of others like it published by CAMRA shows that this interest extends to our pubs as well. Sadly, we continue to lose historic pub interiors at an alarming rate. Mainly this is down to the aforementioned pub closures – about 30 a week in early 2015 - which affect heritage pubs just like any others. However, we also still have owners with no appreciation for or interest in the often precious interiors of which they are now custodians. The article on pages 13 and 14 looks at what can be done to help safeguard the treasures which survive.

11

CAMRA and Pub Heritage

Reception, Berkeley, Scunthorpe

Although CAMRA was initially founded (in 1971) to save Britain's traditional beer, it quickly became clear to campaigners that the best places to drink that beer, our pubs, were also under threat. In due course, CAMRA assigned equal importance to campaigning for real ale and for pubs.

The late 1970s saw a huge increase in the opening out of pubs and removals of fine fittings so preservation of historic pub interiors emerged as a key campaigning issue for CAMRA. After pioneering work in York, a specialist Pub Preservation Group was set up, which evolved into today's Pub Heritage Group. The first step was to identify the most intact interiors surviving across the country's (then) 65,000 pubs. This massive task involved following up thousands of leads, developing criteria for inclusion, recording what was found (both in words and photos) and creating a list – the National Inventory of Historic Pub Interiors (NI). This focuses firstly on interiors which remain largely unaltered since before the second world war, though intact early post-war pubs are also included (but are extremely rare – the Punch Bowl, Worcester (p.114) is the only Midlands example). Secondly, the NI covers pubs with specific features or rooms of national significance (e.g. an intact snug in an otherwise altered pub or examples of especially superb tiling or flamboyant bar backs.)

Punch Bowl, Worcester

The first National Inventory of Historic Pub Interiors appeared in 1997 and totalled 179 entries. Since then it has been continually refined and updated as new candidates were discovered and, sadly, existing entries lost. The present total stands at 270 and full descriptions can be found in our publication, *Britain's Best Real Heritage Pubs*. 51 Midlands pubs are on the NI.

Regional Inventories were the next logical step. As would be expected, the bar for inclusion is set lower than for the NI though the same principles apply, with the emphasis on the internal fabric of the pub and what is authentically old within it. The selection criteria for both National and Regional Inventories are on page 121.

Inventory pubs throughout the country can be found on our website www.heritagepubs.org.uk where clicking on the Search Here facility in the top left-hand corner will take you to easy-to-use drop down menus.

CAMRA is now working on a third tier of Local Inventories. These will describe interiors which have suffered significant damage or change but where vestiges of former glories are still ascertainable.

Pubs in Peril

The current plight of the British pub is only too well known. At the time of going to press, figures show 31 closing each week and, between 1982 and 2014, total pub numbers fell by 20,000. Heritage pubs are in no way exempt from this horrible rate of attrition. Since 2010, five National Inventory pubs in the Midlands have been lost forever whilst another four have been closed for some time and may never reopen. The casualty rate amongst Regional Inventory pubs is even higher.

Crystal Fountain, Cannock, Staffordshire

There are several reasons for this gloomy state of affairs – changing social habits, the impact of the recession, higher prices, the rapacious behaviour of the big pub companies. A particular threat is the attractiveness of many pub buildings to developers. Conversion of rural pubs to houses has been all too common for many years but it's now our urban pubs which are really suffering. Many suburban pubs, for instance, occupy large plots of land, ideal for small supermarkets, and two a week are being lost in that way alone. All this is made worse by our feeble planning laws which allow pubs to be converted to restaurants, shops and most kinds of office without the need for planning consent. CAMRA's Pubs Matter campaign is addressing this problem – please give it your support (www.pubsmatter.org.uk).

This combination of negative factors has posed major problems for urban heritage pubs. Many of them are to be found in unfashionable, off-centre locations where they ticked along for donkey's years,

Woodman, Birmingham

serving the local community. As a result, their owners saw little point investing in the sort of major changes inflicted, in the pursuit of fashion, on many a town or city centre pub so heritage was preserved, more or less by accident. Sadly, though, when the recession began to bite, these pubs tended to drop the wrong side of the profits line – every one of the permanent and long-term closures mentioned earlier is an edge-of-centre or suburban pub.

Historic pubs in peril can, and have been, saved and CAMRA's Pub Heritage Group will fight for every one. One tactic is to draw a threatened pub to the attention of an enlightened small pub company – both the Woodman, Birmingham (p.89), and the Crystal Fountain, Cannock, Staffordshire (p.72), were saved in this way. We also seek to get pubs statutorily listed as this affords them an enhanced degree of protection. (For more on listings, see below).

Where we can, we use the planning system to resist unwanted changes to heritage pubs and encourage local folk to do likewise. Most of all, we aim to generate interest in these precious survivors. Pubs are first and foremost businesses and the more that people use them, the less likely are they to wither and die. You can do your bit by putting this guide to active use.

Statutory Listing

A Short Guide

Hatch, Sun, Leintwardine, Herefordshire

All parts of the United Kingdom have systems for protecting buildings of special architectural or historic interest. The process is devised not to *prevent* change but to *manage* it effectively, working with the grain of the building, not against it. Many of the pubs in this guide are statutorily listed and several have benefited from exemplary refurbishments or extensions where their listed status has ensured careful control. In turn, this has protected their futures as businesses, as without the changes, their viability might have been questionable. Examples are the Sun, Leintwardine, Herefordshire (p.32), the Crystal Fountain, Cannock, Staffordshire (p.72), and the Test Match, West Bridgford, Nottinghamshire (p.62).

In England, listings are made by the Secretary of State for Culture, Media and Sport, on the advice of English Heritage.

Grade I. This highest of gradings covers just 2.5% of all listed buildings: these are those that have 'exceptional', even international interest.
Grade II* (spoken of as 'Two Star'). Covers a further 5.5% of listed buildings. They have 'outstanding' interest.
Grade II. 92% of all English listed buildings are at this grade. They have what is described as 'special' architectural or historic interest.

Most listed pubs are designated at Grade II. The only 'Two Star' pubs in this guide are the magnificent Bartons Arms, Birmingham (p.83), the inter-war gem that is the Test Match, West Bridgford, Nottinghamshire (p.62), the Olde Gate, Brassington, Derbyshire (p.16), and the historic Greyhound & Punchbowl, Bilston, West Midlands (p.83).

Derbyshire

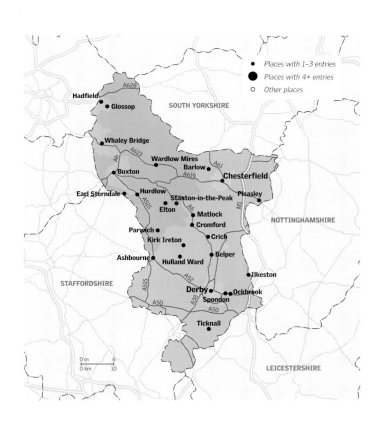

Places with 1–3 entries
Places with 4+ entries
Other places

Hadfield
Glossop
SOUTH YORKSHIRE
Whaley Bridge
Wardlow Mires
Barlow
Buxton
Chesterfield
Hurdlow
Earl Sterndale
Stanton-in-the-Peak
Pleasley
Elton
Matlock
NOTTINGHAMSHIRE
Parwich
Cromford
Kirk Ireton
Crich
Ashbourne
Belper
Hulland Ward
Ilkeston
STAFFORDSHIRE
Derby
Ockbrook
Spondon
Ticknall
LEICESTERSHIRE

0 m   6
0 km   10

Ashbourne

The Butchery, 15 Victoria
Square, DE6 1GG
01335 347387
Grade II listed
LPA: Derbyshire Dales

Horns

A splendid, multi-roomed pub, tucked away down a short alley off the
Market Place. The small public bar to the right of the entrance has an
old bar counter (but modern top), 1930s fireplace and old dado
panelling on one wall. Steps take you down to the split-level rear bar
but the 'must see' is the room to the centre-left. Here, the Minton-tiled
floor was uncovered only recently and the old beams are impressive.
Another room lies beyond the back-to-back fireplace - although small,
it was once two rooms.

Barlow

32 Commonside Road, S18 7SJ

0114 289 0464

Unlisted

LPA: North East Derbyshire

Hare & Hounds

Although much modified in the mid-to-late 1950s, this pub has now gained the charm and patina of what the motor trade likes to call an older restoration. The two front downstairs rooms and an old rear extension form the core and share an irregular quadrilateral servery which has picture window service to all bars. In the L-shaped top room on the right, the fixtures (as elsewhere) are not exactly of great quality, e.g. the Formica bar top, but such period features are becoming rare - likewise the sliding door to the small bar next door and, elsewhere, the tiled fireplaces, leatherette fixed seating and, in the back room, the counter with a copper top.

Belper

29 Chesterfield Road,

DE56 1FF

01773 825525

Unlisted

LPA: Amber Valley

Queens Head

Set in a terrace on the edge of town, this drinkers' pub retains three of its original four rooms and, unusually, seems to have had two off-sales hatches. On the right is the snug with simple bench seating. A further room on the far right and the adjacent quarry-tiled passage have been combined though the original fixed seating survives. More old seating can be found in the quarry-tiled bar to the left and in the lounge at the back. The three bar counters for the central servery are, however, replacements from around 1990.

Brassington

Well Street,

DE4 4HJ

01629 540448

Grade II* listed

LPA: Derbyshire Dales

Olde Gate

A most characterful stone-built pub of 1616, much altered in 1874 and with various minor changes since. The main bar on the right has a truly timeless feel with its pewter mugs hanging from the beams and an old ticking clock. Superb features include the inglenook fireplace with cast-iron range, quarry-tiled flooring and old benches and scrubbed-top tables. The bar arrangements were altered around 1953 when the larger left-hand opening was created (the original hatch is on the right) but the old frontage is still there and likewise the lower part of the bar back and the shelves next to the off-sales hatch. The other room on the right has an inter-war parquet floor and

Main bar, Olde Gate

is fully panelled, the majority of this woodwork possibly even dating back to the 1616 build. The fire surround looks to be inter-war and replaced the now covered-up original on the east side. The room on the left used to be a kitchen and entered pub use around 1952. The high-backed settle came from the nearby Queen Adelaide, Snelston Common, when it shut in 2001.

Buxton

41 High Street, SK17 6HB
01298 23278
Grade II listed
LPA: High Peak

Swan

Three small rooms surround a central servery which has good bar screens with leaded glass; the lower portion seems to have been rebuilt in situ. The rooms comprise a bar with 1960s panelling, a rear smoke room and a 'Scottish-style' lounge with tartan decor, notable fireplaces and a large malt whisky collection. The entrance lobby has glazing over the panel work but the off-sales has disappeared. The gents' boasts a lovely set of three brown urinals.

Chesterfield

1 The Shambles, S40 1PX
01246 237700
Grade II listed
LPA: Chesterfield

Royal Oak

A most attractive town-centre pub, made up of two distinct parts - the 16th-century half-timbered building above was incorporated into

the rest of the pub in the mid 19th century. This top part houses a very small high-ceilinged bar with a 1950s bar counter (but newer top) and fixed seating from (probably) the 1930s. Note the small Royal Oak stained glass panels high up in the outside windows. The lower, larger bar was the original inn and once had two rooms; the bar fittings are about 50 years old. Back in 1967, the pub was scheduled for demolition because of a huge redevelopment scheme. An outcry led to a proposal to hoist the building onto rollers and move it to a new site. Thankfully, neither plan came to fruition.

Top bar,
Royal Oak

Crich

Cliffside, Cromford Road,
DE4 5DP
01773 852444
Grade II listed
LPA: Amber Valley

Cliff

This three-storey gritstone pub may well have been a quarryman's cottage when built around 1800. Last refitted in the 1960s, it has changed little since. You enter past an off-sales hatch then, to the left, go into a small lounge bar; this seems to have been enlarged in the refit by absorbing a rear passageway, hence the wide arch cut into the wall. As with many a 1960s scheme, the bar counter is fronted in stone while the bar back, with its glass shelves, is also very much of the era. The brick fireplace and fixed seating date from this time as well and even the red Formica tables survive. On the right, service to the little Tramway Room is via a small hatch with double windows and a stone counter front. More 1960s features can be found here, including a Tudor arch-shaped ceramic fireplace.

Cromford
47 Cromford Hill, DE4 3RF
01629 822102
Grade II listed
LPA: Amber Valley

Bell

Around 1800 this pub was added on to a terrace of houses built in 1776-7. These, however, aren't any ordinary old houses - they were the first to be erected by Richard Arkwright to accommodate textile workers at his pioneering Cromford Mill and also have workshop space running the whole length of the top floor. The Bell itself has not changed much in 50 years. The tiny snug, accessed from Cromford Hill, has a quarry-tiled floor, old fixed seating and service from a hatch - there was an off-sales hatch in this area until 2009. The old benches in the public bar still display their maker's labels (T. Greaves & Co.) but the bar counter in here is modern. The lounge on the left has its own entrance and was created from a private sitting room in the 1950s; many of the fittings (counter, fixed seating, fireplace) date from that time.

Derby, City Centre
6-7 Queen Street, DE1 3DL
01332 267711
Grade II listed
LPA: Derby

Open Thursday-Saturday evenings

Olde Dolphin Inne ★

Derby's oldest pub occupies a late 16th-century building but is 'Olde' only up to a point - since the splendid interior dates from an inter-war restoration, as does the 'Brewer's Tudor' timbering outside. A corridor passes right through the building with the four bars off to the left clustered round an L-shaped servery. The main bar, front left, has a quarry-tiled floor; at a slightly higher level beyond it is a 'better' room (hence the bell-pushes). Its name, Offiler's Lounge, commemorates the Derby brewery which owned the pub. Next up is a comfortably appointed lounge with large brick fireplace, then, finally, a cosy snug. This has a part-glazed partition wall to the servery, full-height oak panelling and service from a hatch to the bar. Upstairs, the '1530AD Steak Bar' is worth a visit for its massive 16th-century timbers (slightly later than 1530!) and very old brick fireplace with brass hood.

The four bars at the Olde Dolphin were refitted in 'Brewers' Tudor' style during the inter-war years. This is the lounge. The small counter is part of the central servery which is linked to all four rooms

The Olde Dolphin snug, with a hatch to the servery, is an appealing, cosy space

Derby, Normanton
74 Silver Hill Road, DE23 6UJ
01332 342902
Unlisted
LPA: Derby

Lounge, Falstaff

Falstaff

Built in 1886 as a six-bedroom hotel, the Falstaff was designed by Derby architect James Wright for local wine merchants Pountain, Giradot & Forman. 1933 saw a switch to pub operation with some inevitable rearrangement. The public bar still has its Victorian bar counter and fine bar back, the latter in two sections. Part of the wall was removed to enable access to the original off-sales area. In the rear bar, with its old bench seating, you can make out the position of the original bar counter before replacement post-war. The wall to the former living room at the back has gone and this area now houses a pool table. The hotel front door formerly led to the main reception room with the residents' lounge on the right; the wall between them was taken out in 1933 and a small curved counter inserted in one corner. The current bar counter is from the 1990s but the fixed seating and fireplace are Victorian.

Derby, Normanton
Village Street, DE23 8DF
01332 766329
Unlisted
LPA: Derby

Norman Arms

A reasonably intact inter-war 'Brewer's Tudor' pub built on the site of an earlier one. In the front bar, the panelled counter and stone-arched fireplace are as-built, likewise the lower portion of the bar back and the decorative woodwork above the staff doorway. Other features are more recent. The lounge was extended backwards, perhaps in the 1960s, but the front part retains its fielded panelling with decorative strapwork - there is also decoration (three arches) in the panelling above the fine inter-war fireplace. The ladies' stained glass door panel is original but must have been moved, given its position in the extension. Both gents' toilets sport original urinals and terrazzo floors.

Earl Sterndale
SK17 0BU
01298 83211
Unlisted
LPA: High Peak

Quiet Woman

This simple, stone-built pub evolved from a farmhouse or cottages many moons ago. On the left, the public bar has an old counter and bench seating, modern fireplace and panelling and bar-back shelving of indeterminate vintage. The Marston's mirror and undertaker's laying-down table are worthy of note. A small room on the right serves as the lounge; it has a parquet floor, fireplace and dado panelling probably all dating from the 1930s. The unusual small canted panelled counter, surmounted by a glass-fronted display case, looks to be from the 1960s. The pub sign is splendidly incorrect, both politically and grammatically.

Elton
Main Street, DE4 2BW
01629 650367
Grade II listed
LPA: Derbyshire Dales

Opens 8.45pm, also 12-3 Sunday

The public bar at the back of the totally unspoilt Duke of York – a classic among rural pubs

Duke of York ★

Unspoilt pubs of this simplicity, catering only for the wet trade, are very hard to find nowadays. Although minor changes happened in 1985, most of the Victorian interior within this 200-year-old building survives. A central tiled corridor leads to the main bar, entered through a timber partition wall. It has a quarry-tiled floor, fixed bench seating, wood-panelled ceiling, stone fireplace and unusual full-height draught screens each side of the door. The bar counter was extended to the window in 1985, albeit using existing panels. Left off the corridor, a plain pool room has a Victorian tiled fireplace and modern hatch to the servery. On the right is a further simply-appointed room still with its old fixed bench seating. Upstairs is a large club room. The loos are outside, with old pigsties beyond.

Glossop
142 Victoria Street, SK13 8JF
01457 862824
Unlisted
LPA: High Peak

Crown Inn ★

An end-of-terrace traditional local with a little-altered four-room interior, the Crown was built in the 1840s and refitted both in later Victorian and inter-war times. Beyond the porch lies a lobby bar with an unusually ornamented bar counter and two sets of bar-back shelves, both of which could be Victorian but perhaps later (the

mirror in the bar back blocking an outside window suggests a change at some time). Three rooms lead off the lobby, starting with the front snug, still with its inter-war fixed seating and tiled fireplace. The rear snug was a living room until the 1960s but is fitted out in suitably traditional style. The long, spacious games room to the left has fixed seating curving round it but has suffered removal of its fireplace. The three bracket-shaped features round the walls are air vents (with cast-iron grilles outside).

Lounge, Crown Inn

Hadfield
133 Station Road, SK13 1AA
01457 852459
Unlisted
LPA: High Peak

Palatine

A stone-built early 19th-century hotel which was sold to Robinsons Brewery in 1920 and retains much of a refurbishment that took place just after that. The lobby bar has inter-war panelling all around; the bar back with bevelled mirrored panels appears to be 1930s as does

Old bench seating and the inter-war counter at the Palatine

the bar counter in overlaid wood style but it has a new top. To the left are two small rooms – the front one retains old bench seating but has new panelling; the rear one has a hatch to the bar, but modern seating and fireplace. The long front room still has the odd bell-push from the days of table service: the bell-box indicating which room required service is still in place on the wall opposite the bar (see p.28).

Hulland Ward
On A517, DE6 3EE
01335 370206
Unlisted
LPA: Derbyshire Dales

Black Horse

Once a farmhouse, this pub is largely unaltered since 1960. The entrance takes you into a quarry-tiled passage created by a settle on the right. The old public bar is a gem, with its floor laid in an unusual striped pattern of black and red tiles. The settle has bench seating attached, as do the walls. Both bar counter and bar back, with small glass pieces, are from the early 1960s. Further on, the small room on the right has a similar counter and was a kitchen until about 40 years ago. The stone counter in the rear 'Whine Bar' is of the same vintage and there is also old dado panelling. To the left of the public bar another small room has no period features while the large bar on the car park side was converted from a barn in 1960, from when many of the fittings must date.

Hurdlow
Ashbourne Road, SK17 9QQ
01298 83348
Unlisted
LPA: High Peak

Bull i' th' Thorn

Don't be put off by the fake half-timbered frontage of this elevated, rambling pub - inside is a genuine medieval panelled lounge. This small, beamed room has a flagstone floor (under the carpet), full-height panelled walls and an old stone fireplace with copper interior.

Antique items include an ornately carved chair of 1618 which belonged to the Earl of Devonshire and a grandfather clock dated 1742. It opens to a small flagstoned area whose bar counter was probably added when Robinsons bought the pub in 1945. Another small flagstoned room, used for pool, has an old fireplace and panelling which may date from the 1960s. The other four rooms hold little of heritage interest.

The panelled lounge at the Bull i' th' Thorn has medieval origins

---

Ilkeston
24 Station Street, DE7 5TE
0115 932 9684
Unlisted
LPA: Erewash

Dewdrop

Built in 1884 and formerly the Middleton Hotel, the Dewdrop's current layout dates from a 1950s refit. The light oak counter in the public bar is very much a product of that time as are the two-part mirrored bar back and leatherette fixed seating with baffle by the door. The large quarry-tiled lobby has a servery with a sliding hatch

(still operational but locked in the open position) and windows either side plus a 1950s counter front. Note the memorial to Sir Barnes Wallis who slept here during the Second World War. Off the lobby is a children's room with old fixed seating, reclaimed brick fireplace and unfortunate fake half-timbering. Yet another 1950s counter and bar back in the lounge but the fireplace has come from elsewhere.

The drinking passage at the Dewdrop has a 1950s counter and counter screens

Kirk Ireton

Main Street, DE6 3JP
01335 370306
Grade II* listed
LPA: Amber Valley

Servery, Barley Mow

Makeney

Holly Bush Lane, DE56 0RX
01332 841729
Grade II listed
LPA: Amber Valley

Vintage curved partitioning creates the splendid central snug at the Holly Bush

Barley Mow

A 17th-century stone building with mullioned windows, the Barley Mow became an inn some 200 years ago. The undisturbed layout owes much to previous landlady Mrs Ford, who spent all her 89 years here and refused all things modern such as VAT and going decimal. On her death in 1976, her relatives sold the contents (apart from some fixed seating in the bar) so present landlady Mary Short was obliged to buy new furnishings - though these, such as the slate-topped tables, match the interior perfectly. The small low-beamed public bar, with its huge fireplace, exudes traditional atmosphere, heightened by service being via a small counter which is more like a hatch. Casks of beer are stillaged behind the bar and one beer is kept in the cellar and served via a jug - a great rarity nowadays. A passage beyond narrow doors takes you to a small parlour, not brought into regular pub use until 1976. Up a short flight of steps to the right of the servery is the former kitchen, pressed into pub service at busy times.

Holly Bush Inn ★

A marvellous village pub which, like many others, has grown from a small original core. Here this was the superb central snug, formed by a quadrant-shaped partition wall with glazing above and a double-hinged door in the middle. Benches are attached inside, focusing on the fireplace which houses a cast-iron range, albeit dating only from the 1990s. This wonderful space, fully enclosed when the door is shut, has a quarry-tiled floor that extends into the corridor. Here, a diagonal line in a corner near the snug supposedly marks the site of a

counter where beer was served from jugs brought from the cellar prior to the present servery being created in the right-hand room (though Pedigree is still served from a jug kept on the bar back). This room has not changed significantly in the last 50 years, but the windows facing the lean-to extension are modern - the scars of the replaced single window are still visible. The left-hand room took its present form in 1981 when Holly Bush Cottage, beyond the central post, was incorporated into the pub. The inn sign is painted on the frontage - a once common, but now rare, sight.

Matlock Bank
48 Jackson Road, DE4 3JQ
01629 580295
Unlisted
LPA: Derbyshire Dales

Thorn Tree

Situated high above the town, this late 19th-century stone-built pub retains a traditional layout of entrance passage with off-sales ahead and small bars left and right. The distinctive dado panelling on most of the walls dates from a refit of about 1965 which is also when the servery was brought forward from the cellar steps. Little has changed since. The left-hand room has a chunky 1960s bar counter, fixed seating of the same era and a bar back of mixed vintage. In the other bar, the sloping counter and bar-back fittings are from the 1965 refurb but the tiled fireplace is of the 1930s.

Ockbrook
Green Lane, DE72 3SE
01332 662378
Unlisted
LPA: Erewash

The snug has a tiny hatch to the servery (just right of the doorway)

Royal Oak

A pub since 1865, this excellent establishment last saw significant alterations in the mid-1950s. From the front door, a ply-panelled passage with old settle leads to the public bar. This has a classic 1950s bar counter and the two sections of bar back with Formica shelves were added at the same time. The fine tap room (see p.87), front left, has a quarry-tiled floor, old (but re-upholstered) fixed seating and a 1950s tiled fireplace. Another delightful room, the tiny snug, is on the right - it has an appropriately sized hatch to the servery and leatherette-covered fixed seating. The lounge at the back was doubled in size in 1999 but the original front section has what looks like an inglenook fireplace. To the rear left, the Assembly Room was added in 1911. The same family has run the pub since 1953.

Parwich

Chestnut Cottages, DE6 1QL
01335 390212
Unlisted
LPA: Derbyshire Dales

The public bar retains
its inter-war fixed
seating but the bar
fittings are
replacements

Sycamore

The Sycamore occupies a 17th-century building with a late Victorian brick extension. The public bar has inter-war fixed seating but the counter and bar back are recent. The hatch in the servery was for off-sales. Behind the bar, two small rooms are in the oldest part of the

building. One has a hatch to the back of the bar and more inter-war seating while the other has older seating plus an inter-war fireplace with newer brick infill. Since closure of the village shop in 2008, a fourth room (small and quarry-tiled) has contained a well-stocked shop.

Pleasley

Chesterfield Road, NG19 7PA
01623 810235
Unlisted
LPA: Bolsover

Nags Head

A Hardy & Hansons pub of 1935, built behind the original, hence the distance from the road. On the left, the original public bar is only opened for occasional functions while the off-sales further left is intact but unused. The bar in the middle is now the main room and has two sets of 1930s fixed bench seating with a bell-push. The present counter replaced a hatch in the 1960s. A passageway, rear right, has a dado of brown tiles and gives access to the nearly intact toilets. The smoke room (on the right) retains its original fireplace and bench seating - the counter is probably also from 1935, but the bar back is at least partly more recent. Throughout the pub the leaded-glass doors are original and have kept their room numbers, except the right-hand bar where the 3 has gone awol.

Spondon

Potter Street, DE21 7LH
01332 674203
Grade II listed
LPA: Derby

Malt Shovel ★

This largely 18th-century red-brick building houses an impressive, traditional multi-room pub with off-sales, drinking passageway and three other public rooms. The snug is especially interesting, being formed by a full-height, part-glazed curved partition wall with seating attached - one of very few such spaces to survive (the Holly Bush Inn, Makeney, (p.23) being another). Like the corridor, it has a red and black quarry-tiled floor. The small room further down the corridor has old movable benches.

Snug, Malt Shovel

On the right, the lounge is unusual in being accessed across a corner of the servery but otherwise contains little of heritage interest. The large Tudor or Long Room at the front was in use by 1939, though the Tudorisation was mostly done after 1960. The various rooms are identified by letters on the doors, rather than the customary numbers. The kitchen occupies the former brewhouse which ceased activity in 1918.

Stanton-in-the-Peak
Main Street, DE4 2LW
01629 636333
Grade II listed
LPA: Derbyshire Dales

Flying Childers

The pub occupies a late 18th-century gritstone building with a 19th-century extension and its unusual name celebrates a famous racehouse owned by the 4th Duke of Devonshire of nearby Chatsworth House. The inner porch, with red quarry-tiled floor and ply-panelled dado, has an off-sales window. On the right is the very small snug bar with old bar-back shelves but a recent counter. The fireplace and settle seating are probably 1930s. The lounge on the left was formerly two cottages and came into pub use around 1950. Apart from the fireplace, most fittings are from that era or a bit later. Outside, the initials WPT in the doorway lintels refer to William Paul Thornhill of Stanton Hall - the family still owns the pub.

Ticknall
27 High Street, DE73 7JH
01332 864392
Grade II listed
LPA: South Derbyshire

Chequers

Much of what we see inside this 17th-century pub derives from a refit in the early 1950s. In the main room, both bar counter and bar back are typical of that time, the latter with small drawers still used as a till. A settle formerly almost encircled the inglenook fireplace but most was removed in 1968 so only a tiny portion remains. Seats either side of the fireplace have headroom scooped out of the breast beam. A second, small room has old dado panelling, 1950s brick fireplace and a piano which is still played on Saturday nights. A third room marked private can see use at busy times. Sadly, the 50-year-old egg-throwing competition on Easter Monday was stopped in 2003 on health and safety grounds.

Wardlow Mires
A623, SK17 8RW
01298 872268
Grade II listed
LPA: Derbyshire Dales

Open 7-11 Friday, 12-11 Saturday,
Sunday and bank holidays

Three Stags Heads ★

This remote country pub on the A623 used to be part of a farm but is now linked to a pottery business. The entrance leads to the basic main bar with a stone-flagged floor and huge stone fire surround. The counter was installed in the 1940s (the front is 1980s) along with the brown painted shelves which serve as a back-fitting. To the right is the 'Music Room', only recently brought into pub use but kitted out in a style which fully matches the rustic spirit of the main bar. The door

on the left of the lobby, with a figure 3 on it, is to the original second public room and is pressed into service when the pub is busy. The Abbeydale beers include the ferocious Lurcher (8%), brewed only for the pub and celebrating its dog-friendliness.

Public bar, Three Stags Head

Whaley Bridge
7 Old Road, SK23 7HR
01663 732384
Unlisted
LPA: High Peak

Shepherds Arms

On entering this stone-built former farmhouse, you encounter the six-foot-square 'Lift Shaft', perhaps the smallest pub room in Derbyshire. However, the star attraction lies beyond on the right - the splendid flagstone-floored tap room. Old features here include the bar counter, two sets of fixed wooden seating, two oblong scrubbed tables and a cupboard in the wall. The replacement fireplace (2009)

is in keeping with the traditional atmosphere and only the modern bar-back shelves strike a jarring note. A flagstone passage runs along the back of this room from an outside door on the right and a window between the tap room and lounge entrances suggests a former off-sales. The lounge was previously two small rooms and only the dado panelling is not recent.

Public bar and regulars at the Shepherds Arms

Table Service

A man walks into a pub. He wants a drink. What does he do? Simple, he goes to the bar, orders it, pays for it and enjoys it. Few of us would ever think that things were otherwise, but they were. And the clues are there! If you visit some of the multi-room pubs in this guide you will see what look like door bells. You won't find them in the public bar but you will in the 'better class' rooms, such as the lounge, saloon or smoke room where customers expected to pay a shade more for their drinks in return for somewhat smarter surroundings.

Bell box, Palatine, Hadfield, Derbyshire

Adding to the sophistication was the chance of being served at your table, something that would make you feel good about yourself and impress your wife or girlfriend (escorted women were welcome in the better rooms of pub). You pressed the bell and it rang in the serving area and the barman or a waiter would come and get your order (a small tip seems to have been the order of the day). The bells were usually linked to an indicator box which showed where service was required.

An alternative method providing table service came home to the present writer, when after starting my drinking career as a sixth-former in Birmingham in the early 1960s, a move to Manchester provided a new experience where waiters moved around the pub taking orders. As far as a I know, such a practice seemed to have disappeared in Brum by that time. Maybe some readers can tell otherwise.

Table service has all but disappeared in the UK but is still practised at one pub in this guide, the Peacock, Nottingham (p.58), where, except on Friday or Saturday night, you can sit down in the lounge bar, press one of the bell-pushes and get served. Apart from table service at a number of the new breed of micro-pubs, it is also to be found at the National Inventory-listed Volunteer Canteen, Waterloo, Merseyside, and the Clep Bar, Dundee (for both see www.heritagepubs. org.uk).

A curious thing about bell-pushes is their geography. They are common from the Midlands and northwards but are very rare to the south. It is impossible to conjecture why this is so since we know that waiter service was commonplace in many London pubs a century ago. We would be

Lounge, Peacock, Nottingham

most interested to hear of examples south of, say, Coventry (info.pubheritage@camra.org.uk) .

The moral of this story for our man who goes into a pub – don't do what you are expected to do on the continent and sit down waiting to be served. It won't happen. The bell-push and the days of table service in the British pub are long gone, although a few of our smarter bars seem to bringing back the tradition – good for them.

Geoff Brandwood

Herefordshire

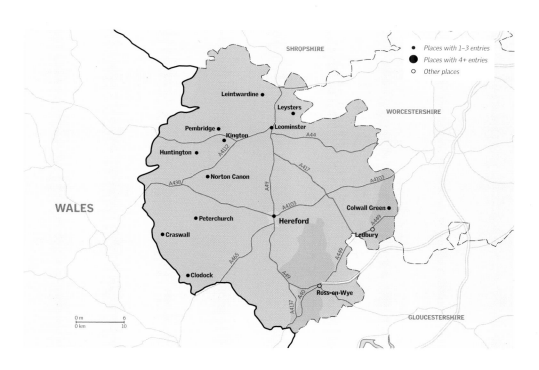

SHROPSHIRE

Places with 1–3 entries
Places with 4+ entries
Other places

WORCESTERSHIRE

Leintwardine

Leysters

Pembridge
Kington
Leominster
A44

Huntington

A4112

Norton Canon

A417

A438

A49

A4103

WALES

A4103

Colwall Green

Peterchurch
Hereford

Craswall

A449

Ledbury

A465

A449

Clodock

A49

Ross-on-Wye

A40

A4137

GLOUCESTERSHIRE

0 m   6
0 km   10

Clodock
HR2 0PD
01873 860677
Grade II listed
LPA: Herefordshire

Cornewall Arms

A rare example of an unspoilt village pub with no music, no TV, no fruit machine and no food - but good conversation. A pub since 1870, it once had a butcher's shop and slaughterhouse attached. On the left of a flagstone passage, there is a servery at a much lower level. It has old bar fittings and service through a hatch, with a window now open permanently and a Formica shelf. The bar comprised two rooms until 1960 when a wall was replaced with a wooden partition (always folded back nowadays). At the front is a flagstone floor, superb curved high-back settle, 1920s bentwood 'holey' seat and an old fireplace (with 1980s infill). The rear section features half-ply panelled walls and a modern fireplace with old mirror surround above. A venerable skittle table is always ready for play.

29

Colwall Green
Walwyn Road, WR13 6ED
01684 540498
Unlisted
LPA: Herefordshire

Yew Tree

This old pub was fully refitted in the late 1950s by Cheltenham & Hereford Breweries Ltd, using oak fittings by Worcester Woodcraft. Both rooms and the tiny off-sales hatch have barely changed since, though a Formica top was fixed on one bar counter in the 1970s. The counters, bar backs, upholstered fixed seating and fireplaces are, though, untouched.

The right-hand room at the Yew Tree still has the counter and bar back as installed in the late 1950s

Craswall
HR2 0PN
01981 510616
Unlisted
LPA: Herefordshire

Bulls Head

The public bar is the star at this 18th-century farmhouse pub (although the farm was sold off in 1997). Two ancient stone steps take you down to the small flagstone-floored room which retains several old features - the stone fireplace, the lovely stove and three settles, one of them high-backed. Service is from two small hatches cut into the wall to the cellar - the right-hand one replaced a door in 1997. The cellar servery has ancient bar-back shelves and casks on a stillage. The former purpose of the Doulton sink in the front window is unknown but cyclists now find it useful for filling their water bottles! Up well-worn steps on the left and through a low doorway is the second original room, now used for dining. It has a flagstone floor, beamed ceiling and old stone fireplace but the food counter is a recent intrusion. The third room on the left came into pub use quite recently. Please note: this pub is currently operating only as a restaurant and that opening hours are limited.

Hereford
36 Grandstand Street,
HR4 9NF
01432 275785
Unlisted
LPA: Herefordshire

Food Sunday lunchtimes only

Golden Lion

In 1938 the adjoining house (left of the pub) was incorporated into a much enlarged public bar and many fittings remain from then. An intact off-sales remains in the lobby. Through a door partition on the left is the public bar – note there are Victorian-style 'Public Bar' etched windows in both parts, so that on the left has been moved (or is a copy). A new Formica frontage was added to the counter in the 1980s. On the right the lounge/dining room has a counter that may date from the 1950s but it too has front panels added in the 1980s and the top looks to be of similar date; the bar-back fitting is post-war.

The off-sales compartment at the Golden Lion is a rare survivor

Hereford
111 Widemarsh Street,
HR4 9EZ
07736 714823
Grade II listed
LPA: Herefordshire

Left-hand bar, Oxford Arms

Oxford Arms

A 17th-century timber-framed building, last refitted in the 1930s. The off-sales hatch remains intact in the entrance porch. Inside, the small bars to the left and right both have 1930s bar backs and panelled counter fronts (with new tops) while the left-hand room also has its 1930s fireplace. The room to the rear-right came into pub use more recently. Look for the old bell-box within the servery of the lounge.

Huntington
HR5 3PY
01544 370656
Unlisted
LPA: Herefordshire

Only open Tuesday to Sunday evenings

Swan

Unchanged since a refit in the 1950s, this 17th-century cottage pub is blissfully free of such new-fangled gimmicks as TV, pool or fruit machines (or a juke box - removed by the present owners). In the quarry-tiled public bar, the counter front incorporates 17th-century panelling from an old chest and the bar-back shelves are topped with more such panelling. A big old stone fireplace, settle and quoits complete the scene. The lounge on the right has a 'front room' ambience. There are ply panels in an old counter, a Welsh dresser for a bar back, a venerable fireplace, settle and a grandfather clock.

Kington

22 Victoria Road, HR5 3BX
01544 239033
Grade II listed
LPA: Herefordshire

The unspoilt Victorian public bar

Ye Olde Tavern ★

The Jones family owned this pub from 1884 to 2002 and, thankfully, did little to change it over the years. You enter by a lobby, still with its off-sales facility. The small public bar, to the left, is the chief interest here. It retains a Victorian or very early 20th-century feel thanks to the simple fittings - high counter, bar back, fixed seating, panelling, and a built-in cupboard next to the (probably) inter-war fireplace. Right of the lobby, the second room, with flagstone floor and service via a stable door, once housed a mighty settle. Sadly this was destroyed in 2002 to create more trading space but its footprint survives. At the rear, what was a third room became toilets in 2002.

Leintwardine

Rosemary Lane, SY7 0LP
01547 540705
Grade II listed
LPA: Herefordshire

Sun Inn ★

This pub was kept for 74 years by Florence (Flossie) Lane, whose family took it over early in the 20th century. She died in 2009 a month shy of her 95th birthday and so legendary had both she and her utterly unspoilt pub become that obituaries appeared in *The Times* and *Daily Telegraph*. The pub, occupying part of a row of early 19th-century cottages, had been trading since at least the 1860s and

was one of the last remaining beerhouses (Flossie only introduced wine in later years). In her time, right of the entrance lobby, was the 'Brick Bar' (named after the flooring material), equipped with basic tables and benches and a (probably) 1950s brick fireplace. Left of the entrance was 'Flossie's Room', the parlour where she sat, and beyond that, a ground-floor cellar where, in later years, regulars served

Flossie's Room

themselves and put their payment in a tin. New ownership has seen all this scrupulously preserved but, in the interests of viability, a large, though very well-designed extension (with bar counter), was opened in 2011 with access through the old lobby.

Leominster
2 Broad Street, HR6 8BS
01568 611404
Grade II listed
LPA: Herefordshire

Grape Vaults

A small 19th-century town-centre pub with an almost intact three-room layout and a fair number of features from the early 1900s. The fittings include plenty of old tongue-and-groove half-height-panelling, wall-benches, fireplaces and bar counter but the bar back is a replacement. The tiny room rear left is separated from the rest of the pub by a part-glazed partition.

The public bar

Leysters
HR6 0HW
01568 750230
Unlisted
LPA: Herefordshire

Duke of York ★

Modest and beautifully kept, this country pub still has a smallholding attached and has been in the hands of the same family since 1911. The interior, little altered since before the Second World War, comprises three rooms. The public bar has a fine, curved, high-backed settle (which predates 1911) beside the fireplace and simple dado panelling. Beneath the window, a bench is equipped for the local version of quoits - four quoits a go, five points for the pin, two for the inner ring and one for the outer (but they must land white side up). Right is a small darts room with a Victorian tiled fireplace, corner bench and hatch. The lounge on the left was added to the public rooms just before the war and feels like a domestic sitting room.

The well-appointed public bar at the Duke of York has a hatch to the servery and a settle

Norton Canon
HR4 7BH
01544 318375
Unlisted
LPA: Herefordshire

Three Horseshoes

A single-storey, brick-built pub which still has three rooms. On the right is a bar with red quarry-tiled flooring and bar fittings from the 1930s. The lounge on the left has a small bar counter with Formica top, which looks to be more of the 1950s than 1930s, as does the bar back: note the exposed section of wattle and daub on one half-timbered wall. A large pool room at the back doubles as a venue for an air gun league. This is the home of Shoe's Brewery established in 1994.

The public bar at the Three Horseshoes has a bar counter dating from the 1930s

Pembridge
Market Square, HR6 9DZ
01544 388427
Grade II listed
LPA: Herefordshire

New Inn

The public bar of this fine 17th-century half-timbered building boasts a superb settle, inglenook fireplace and a pair of handpumps against the wall (suggesting there was no bar counter until quite recently). A stone floor and large stone fireplace complete the picture. In the hall area is what appears to be an old bar back, perhaps removed from elsewhere, while the lounge on the right and restaurant downstairs contain little of heritage interest.

The public bar at the New Inn has a 17th-century beamed ceiling, a long settle and old stone fireplace

Peterchurch

HR2 0SJ
01981 550179
Unlisted
LPA: Herefordshire

Nags Head

Few alterations have taken place at this three-roomed pub since a remodelling in the 1950s. The main, quarry-tiled bar once consisted of two rooms and the fireplace and counter date from the refit. The handpumps are actually dated 1954 but the bar back, with its bevelled mirror panels and sturdy pillars, goes back to Victorian times; sadly, its lower shelving has given way to fridges. Off to the left is a tiny room (the 'Lincoln Suite') with a hatch to the side of the bar. At times up to ten people can be found crowded into here while the rest of the pub stays empty! The dining room has half-height ply-panelling but little else of interest and no doubt entered pub use fairly recently.

Snug, Nags Head

Gents Only

1st January 1976 was a momentous day for women's rights. This was when the Sex Discrimination Act of 1975 came into force, making it illegal, among many other things, to exclude women from all or part of a public house.

Once upon a time it was gents only in this room at the Loggerheads

It exposed the nonsense that many a public house was anything of the sort if it refused to admit half the population to all or some of its bars! Traditionally public bars were always very much a male preserve but the 'better' rooms usually welcomed female customers provided they were accompanied by males or other respectable ladies. Now and again you can still see the odd reminder of the old, unenlightened ways. The best example at a pub in this guide is at the Loggerheads, Shrewsbury (p.66), where, on a baffle at the entrance to the left-hand room, is written the legend 'GENTS ONLY until 1975'. We also know that at the Bell & Cross, Clent, Worcestershire (p.109), there was a men's smoke room. At the mighty Black Horse, Northfield, Birmingham (p.94), a back room there was another gents' smoke room, while at the British Oak, Stirchley, also Birmingham (p.94), there was a single-sex, male space in the lounge at the front left of the pub.

Geoff Brandwood

Leicestershire & Rutland

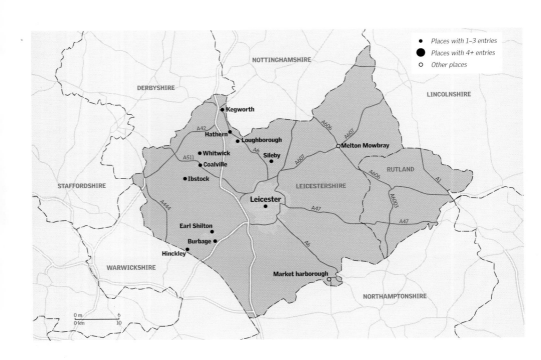

Places with 1–3 entries
Places with 4+ entries
Other places

Burbage

Hinckley Road, LE10 2AF
01455 239443
Unlisted
LPA: Hinckley & Bosworth

The servery in the corridor dates back to the 1930s

Cross Keys

An inter-war refurbishment and extension to an older building

provide most of the interest here. To the left of the entrance is the central servery with quadrant three-light hatch, now minus its sliding sashes. Opposite is a splendid small snug area around a 1930s inglenook fireplace with fixed bench seating and fielded panelling. The area beyond the fireplace was formerly a separate snug but the partition with door was removed quite recently - it too has fixed seating and the odd bell-push. Right of the entrance is a bare-boarded bar with lovely inter-war bench seating and a baffle by the door. The large Art Deco brick fireplaces and bar counter are also probably from the refit though only one of the bar-back fittings (the one holding snacks) is not modern. A long central passage runs to the back of the building and the hatch and shelf for service suggest passageway drinking in the past. The rear lounge/dining room was totally revamped in the last decade.

Coalville
72 High Street, LE67 3EE
01530 833278
Unlisted
LPA: North West Leicestershire

Stamford & Warrington

An excellent and little-changed example of how pubs were refitted in the late 1950s/early 1960s. Just beyond the entrance is an off-sales with sliding window hatch and Formica shelf. The public bar on the right has a lino-tiled floor and plenty of features from the refit - bar counter with ribbed hardboard frontage, period bar back and tiled fireplace, fixed bench seating and tables topped with red Formica. The little-used lounge is on the left, with leatherette bench seating and a hatch-like counter to the back of the servery. Formerly a coaching inn, the pub retains stables behind and a coach arch on the left-hand side. Considering its town-centre position, this is a remarkable survivor.

Earl Shilton
72 Keats Lane, LE9 7DR
01455 842338
Unlisted
LPA: Hinckley & Bosworth

Dog & Gun

The original layout and many fittings have survived well in this 1932 Tudor-style pub. From the porch are an off-sales and doors to the lounge and tap room. The lounge has its original bar counter, bar back, doors and door furniture but only part of the old panelling. The rear door leads into an attractive quarry-tiled and panelled corridor - note the 'Servery' brass plaque on the half door with serving hatch above. The snug at the rear right is the choicest room, retaining its panelling, fixed bench seating and fireplace with panelled surround. It now opens into the tap room where there were alterations to the bar area in the 1970s, mainly the repositioning of the counter. The brick fireplace is original, albeit with 1970s inset, as is the fixed seating. For some reason, the pub once sold vast quantities of liquorice!

The snug, fitted out in 1932

Hathern
49 Loughborough Road,
LE12 5HY
01509 842438
Unlisted
LPA: Charnwood

Dew Drop

The Georgian-style brick frontage was added to this small
19th-century pub in the 1930s, since when there have been few
changes. On entering, you pass the intact off-sales then turn right
into the public bar, which was doubled in size by the 1930s scheme.
The counter here looks inter-war but both the bar back and fireplace
are probably from the 1960s. The tiny lounge has a modern counter
front added to what must previously have been just a hatch. The fixed
seating is from the Thirties alterations but again the fireplace is later.
Both gents' and ladies' have glazed white brick walls.

Hinckley
318 Coventry Road, LE10 0NQ
07815 095442
Unlisted
LPA: Hinckley & Bosworth

Wharf

Another 1930s Tudor-style pub which has suffered relatively little at
the hands of the modernisers. All three small rooms at the front
retain their brick and wood surround fireplaces (now covered by
radiators) but the middle one has lost a partition, opening it up to the

servery area. This room
also has settle-like seating
created by a panelled
partition. The servery in
the centre of the pub has
its original bar counter
whilst the passageway
alongside, with fielded
panelling to picture-frame
height, is a popular
drinking area. In the
larger lounge at the back,
the brick fireplace and
fixed seating are unaltered

The 1930s snug at the Wharf

but not so the bar counter where post-war tinkering is in evidence. A
door on the left-hand side of the pub once led to an off-sales but now
accesses a kitchen.

Ibstock
71 Curzon Street, LE67 6LA
01530 262123
Unlisted
LPA: North West Leicestershire

Waggon & Horses

A Georgian pub whose original two rooms still exist within an
expanded layout. Left of the entrance is the snug, or Mardy Room as
the locals call it. This has a red quarry-tiled floor, Victorian fixed
seating and inset cupboards plus a modern surround to an old
fireplace moved from what is now the pool room. That room, also left
of the corridor, was living quarters, then between the wars, a doctor's
surgery. The third room is the bar with its still-used stove whose flue-
pipe rises up and out of the side of the room - a rare sight indeed.

In the Sixties, ply panels were attached to the bar counter along with a Formica top and the bar back was altered at the same time, only one piece of original ornate fretwork surviving. The ply wall-panelling is also from that period. Features elsewhere include ornate cornices and mouldings in the corridor, sash windows and original doors (with new glass).

Kegworth
139 Station Road, DE74 2FR
01509 672846
Unlisted
LPA: North West Leicestershire

Anchor

Rebuilt in 1934 with a mock-Tudor exterior, the Anchor was barely changed until 2009, when the front rooms were combined; however, there are still many original fittings. The small public bar has a good original copper-topped bar counter, herringbone tiled floor, old fireplace and fixed seating and a bar back comprising just a few shelves. Removal of the wall between this room and the lounge saw two small sections of fixed seating disappear and the front-right door fall out of use. A tiled passage at the rear leads to a splendidly intact gents'. Another small room at the back is served by a hatch and retains its parquet floor and wooden fireplace surround, albeit with an unfortunate 'Victorian' fireplace within. The off-sales is no longer in use but at least intact.

Leicester
Glenfield Road, LE3 6AR
0116 262 1022
Unlisted
LPA: Leicester

Sir Charles Napier

A 1938 brick-built pub, little altered since extensions around 1960. The curved bar counter in the front lounge is probably original, though the top is Sixties Formica. A stone-arched fireplace and the fixed seating also date from 1938 but the bar-back shelves are later, as is the ply wall-panelling. Another original bar counter is to be found in the rear concert room, again with 1960s accretions in the form of leatherette padding plus other changes from that time like the glass bar-back shelves and ply panelling. In the public bar, both bar counter (plain with Formica inlay top) and bar back are from the 1960s when this room was extended into the house next door.

Loughborough
85 Ashby Road, LE11 3AB
01509 263565
Unlisted
LPA: Charnwood

Generous Briton

The only significant changes to the public bar since this pub was rebuilt in 1937 are some panelling work on the bar back and windows refitted in the 1990s. The bar counter, unusual arch-shaped stone fireplace, bench seating and bar-back surround are all original. The lounge combines what were two small rooms and has a similar fireplace to that in the public bar. Other original features are the fielded panelling to picture-frame height and the lower portion of the bar back.

Loughborough

21 The Rushes, LE11 5BE
01509 217014
Unlisted
LPA: Charnwood

The left-hand bar at the
Swan in the Rushes

Swan in the Rushes

A 1932-built town pub (originally the Charnwood Inn) with glazed stone frontage and retaining its two rooms plus lobby layout. The smoke room, to the left of the terrazzo-floored lobby, has an as-built fireplace, parquet floor, fixed seating and baffle with leaded glass. The bar back has seen some changes and the counter has a 1960s look. In the right-hand bar, the counter (with a rare shallow copper trough running round the base) and the fixed seating, with plain baffles at each end, are original. Sadly, the original leaded front windows have given way to modern replacements. A small back room was previously part of the living quarters.

Sileby

54 Swan Street, LE12 7NW
01509 814832
Unlisted
LPA: Charnwood

White Swan

The set-back position of this 1937 pub results from it having replaced an older building. The right-hand passage has an inter-war tiled dado and five of the six doors still have glass panels etched with the room names. The off-sales has become a kitchen but the entrance remains, tucked away on the right. In the bar, the bar back is original but the counters have been replaced and extended into the smoke room and lounge, where the bar back is 1960s/70s. Fixed seating and a baffle in the bar and smoke room are from 1937 but not so the fireplaces - the surround on the lounge fireplace does, though, look genuinely old.

Whitwick

11 Leicester Road, LE67 5GN

01530 837311

Grade II listed

LPA: North West Leicestershire

Three Horseshoes ★

This completely unspoilt local, in a former coal-mining village, is nicknamed 'Polly Burton's' after the current landlady's grandmother who started the business well over a century ago. The 1882 date on the front records when it was created from four cottages. A small entrance lobby, complete with off-sales hatch, leads into the public bar on the left. All-over quarry-tiled flooring and extensive bench seating straddle the two former cottage rooms. The servery fittings and both fireplaces are original and the only change seems to be the boxing-in of the seating in the late 20th century. There is nothing so fancy as a till - the takings are just popped into pint glasses. Right of the lobby, a small snug has a bare wooden floor, Victorian fireplace and basic bench seating; service is from a hatch to the back of the bar servery.

The public bar at the Three Horseshoes runs from the front to the back of the building and has a tiled floor and a Victorian bar counter

Celebrating Ceramics

A very distinctive feature of some of the pubs in this guide is the use of decorative ceramics. Of course, every pub building uses ceramics of one sort or another even if it's just in the loos where they provide hard-wearing, hygienic surfaces for the walls, floors and the sanitary ware. But here we are concerned with the smarter end of the market and, in particular, the golden age of pub-building around 1900.

At the end of the Victorian age and into the early twentieth century, great efforts were made in the direction of pub embellishment as breweries and pub-owners sought to attract customers by providing appealing surroundings. Decorative ceramics were one way of doing this. Some pubs were even provided with tiled paintings and the best place in the Midlands to find them is Birmingham. The Fighting Cocks in Moseley was rebuilt in 1898-9 by Holt's Brewery and has a couple of pictorial scenes, one showing what was presumably the predecessor pub (it's named the Fighting Cocks), the other a village church (entry p.93, photos p.2). The makers were Craven Dunnill of Jackfield, Shropshire, a firm which is still in existence. Across the city, the splendid Mitchells & Butlers' Bartons Arms was going up at the same time as the Fighting Cocks and here Minton Hollins provided the extensive tilework, including a huge hunting scene – not exactly an everyday occurrence in Edwardian Aston (p.83)!

Red Lion, Erdington, Birmingham

Great Yarmouth, they seem to the last tiled paintings installed in a British pub.

Another spectacular use of ceramics in the pub is for bar counters. There are thought to be fourteen of these in the UK and three are to be found in the West Midlands: the Gunmakers Arms (but just a fragment: p.92) and Red Lion, Erdington (p.90), both in Birmingham; and the Horse & Jockey, Wednesbury (p.103).

Full-height wall-tiling adds distinction to the rooms and passages in a number of pubs in this guide and, apart from the Rose Villa Tavern, the following can be singled out: the Bull's Head,

Tiled paintings in pubs were in vogue about 1900 but the Rose Villa Tavern, also for Mitchells & Butlers, has very late examples (p.91). It was built in 1919-20 and its floor-to-ceiling tiling includes a whole

Rose Villa Tavern, Hockley, Birmingham

series of panels showed scantily-clad girls disporting themselves in Arcadian surroundings. The makers were Carters of Poole. Apart from some 1930s examples by Lacons Brewery in

White Swan, Digbeth, Birmingham

Birmingham; Paul Pry, Worcester (p.114); Seven Stars, Stourbridge (p.102). Other more modest use of ceramics included mosaic floors at the entrance to pubs and tiled dadoes. Three West Midlands pubs with splendid tilework ought to find their way into the main body of this guide but sadly they are currently closed. They are the Waterloo, Smethwick, famous for its wonderful tiled basement room (originally a restaurant: p.116); the Red Lion, Handsworth, Birmingham, with tiled walls and a whole series of tile paintings (p.116); and the Market Tavern, Birmingham, with full-height wall-tiling.

Geoff Brandwood

Golden Cup, Hanley, Stoke-on-Trent

Telford, Shropshire (p.68); Swan & Mitre (p.84), White Swan, (p.88), and Woodman (p.89), all in

Taking it Home with You

Where did you last buy a drink to take home? Chances are it was a supermarket, perhaps a convenience store or possibly a high street drinks shop. It's hardly likely to have been down at your local pub. But fifty years ago or more it would

Off-sales hatch, Cliff, Crich, Derbyshire

have been a very different story. Pubs sold drinks of all kinds for customers to enjoy at home and very often there was special provision in the layout of the building to cater for this. Then legislation changed in the early 1960s to enable supermarkets to sell alcohol freely and the rest is history. The 'offie' at the pub is now a thing of the past.

The 'off-sales' at pubs went under a bewildering variety of names: off-sales (of course), jug and bottle (and vice versa), outdoor department, family department, retail department, order department, and so on, and

Etched window, Golden Cup, Stoke-on-Trent

you can sometimes still see the old names fossilised in etched glass or door-plates. Occasionally there was a bench in the space in question: typically this would be occupied by women popping down to get beer for their dad or husband and stopping for a quick one with their friends. Where there was no special enclosed small space for off-sales, there might be a hatch facing the front door or one in a corridor.

With the demise of off-sales from pubs, so many small rooms or compartments devoted to the purpose have been incorporated into another pub room or turned over to storage. So, when next you see what appears to be a spare door on the outside of a pub, ask yourself this question - was this for off-sales?

Geoff Brandwood

Lincolnshire

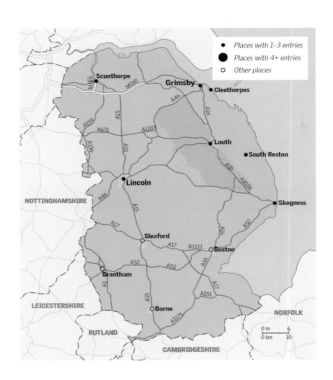

Places with 1–3 entries
Places with 4+ entries
Other places

Balmoral Road, DN35 9ND
01472 698867
Unlisted
LPA: North East Lincolnshire

Crows Nest Hotel

This suburban estate pub of spacious proportions and some quality was built in 1957-8 as a pub-cum-hotel by Samuel Smith's Brewery. The three original pub rooms, planned around a central servery, all have generous fitted seating and deep-windowed bays, giving good natural light. A further lounge bar was created around 1981 from the former hotel dining room (and its toilets) and a new opening, with sliding doors, was formed through to the original lounge. The off-sales became a kitchen some time later. Unspoilt ladies' and gents' toilets off both lobbies.

The snug, Crows Nest Hotel

Grimsby

88 Freeman Street, DN32 7AG
01472 354373
Grade II listed
LPA: North East Lincolnshire

Corporation

Once-proud Victorian town-centre pub which preserves, in its back smoke room, a truly splendid historic interior. This richly ornamented little room, which benefitted from some sensitive refurbishment in 2009, has superb fitted seating and wood panelling

which was originally installed by the Hull furnishing firm of Frederick Eustace (whose fitters' labels are still in situ). The pub's other rooms have been altered considerably but remnants survive of excellent etched and frosted windows. One of the upstairs rooms was used as a music hall in the 1880s.

The grand, panelled Victorian smoke room at the Corporation

Lincoln

18-20 Saltergate, LN2 1DH
01522 262998
Unlisted
LPA: Lincoln

Still

A rather grand pub, occupying part of a large range of early 20th-century buildings constructed for the Co-operative Provident Society. A small, somewhat altered lobby faces the narrow end of the counter and opens into bars left and right. Both the lobby and splendid turned-wood central bar back are surmounted by leaded glass panels to ceiling height. Both bars are panelled but some

matchboarding may be later and the bench seating is modern. Two more lounges can be found to the rear on the right, the smaller retaining its old bench seating and Art Nouveau-style glazed panels.

Right-hand room, Still

Louth

62 Westgate, LN11 9YD
01507 606262
Grade II listed
LPA: East Lindsey

Right bar,
Wheatsheaf

Wheatsheaf

A brick-built pub whose fittings date from several different eras, though there are strong signs of a comprehensive inter-war refurbishment. A flagstone passage runs from the front door to the rear patio. A snug at one end has a separate entrance and inter-war bench seating. The good-quality low panelled counter (possibly

Edwardian) forms part of a square servery, the rest of which features much later fittings. Behind the servery, a small room with an oldish counter is now opened up to a rear lounge housing an inter-war brick fireplace. A further lounge lies across the central corridor - it has chunky bench seating and a curved servery, formerly in the opposite corner of the room.

Scunthorpe

Doncaster Road, DN15 7DS
01724 842333
Unlisted
LPA: North Lincolnshire

Public bar, Berkeley

Berkeley ★

One of the country's best-preserved roadhouses, this local landmark on the outskirts of town will be familiar to generations of trippers to the Lincolnshire coast. Opened in 1940 and designed by West Midlands architects Scott & Clark of Wednesbury, it retains the original layout of three main rooms (one now a dining room), spacious entrance foyer, impressive ballroom and (disused) off-sales. Some fittings have been renewed in recent times by present owners, Samuel Smith, but with the emphasis, as usual with this brewery, on

careful and sympathetic restoration. The foyer and public bar (the latter separately accessed, in keeping with its era) are still largely as-built and, elsewhere in the building, the joinery, ceilings, plasterwork and windows are also mostly original. The main lounge has its original counter, back fitting and bench seating but the entrance screenwork and Art Deco-style lighting are careful re-creations of how they might have appeared in the 1940s. The prominent fireplace, though a genuine Thirties product, is an import from elsewhere.

Scunthorpe
Derwent Road, DN16 2PE
01724 840827
Unlisted
LPA: North Lincolnshire

Queen Bess

A largely intact estate pub built in 1957. From the entrance porch, with its central display bay window, doors go left (lounge) and right (public bar). The former has benches, choice panelling and a curved counter in varnished ply. Only the replacement brick fireplace strikes a jarring note though the inset lighting in the canopy over the servery has also been modernised. The baffle next to the door with its large glass panel is an unusual, if seemingly impractical, feature. The public bar is very plain, with benches on two sides and the original tables and chairs. The counter and bar back are of a curious design. There is a large, plain concert room at the back and the off-sales is intact, albeit out of use.

1950s chic in the public bar at the Queen Bess. Intact 1950s or 1960s pub rooms are now very rare

Scunthorpe
Grange Lane South, DN16 3BJ
01724 840068
Unlisted
LPA: North Lincolnshire

Sherpa

This 1960-vintage pub has an unaltered three-room layout. The lobby is outstanding with its original woodwork, doors and a screen which features mountaineering figures in frosted glass. The large main bar (formerly the concert room) retains its original curved bar counter and bar back. On the left, the smoke room also has relics from the 1960s - the small counter, mirrored bar back, fixed seating, curved bay window and wall-panelling. Also on this side is the lounge, now accessed via the smoke room, again with counter front, bar back and seating intact. The old off-sales can be seen opposite the disused door to the lounge.

Skegness

Vine Road, PE25 3DB

01754 763018

Unlisted

LPA: East Lindsey

Vine Hotel

A late 18th-century hotel which retains much of the character imparted by a 1930s refurbishment. Off the panelled hotel hall is the 'Tennyson Bar' which has an all-round, low-level dado and a very attractive hatch counter with timber apron and surround. A passage leads to the 'Oak Room', which also has a separate entrance through a leaded-glass lobby. This fine room has panelling on all walls, almost to ceiling height and a 1930s brick fireplace, painted an unfortunate shade of maroon. The chunky counter and bar back are of more recent vintage but the tables and chairs probably date to the 1930s refit. Despite the alterations, this is a delightful and atmospheric place. The garden is claimed to be that into which Tennyson invited Maud to come.

The panelled Oak Room at the Vine

South Reston

Main Road, LN11 8JQ

01507 450364

Unlisted

LPA: East Lindsey

Waggon & Horses

A 1930s Tudor-style roadhouse built for Hewitt's Brewery of Grimsby, as can be seen from the stained and leaded windows in each of the original front rooms. That three-room layout is still clearly discernible but wide arches have replaced the doors (and with a

puzzling change of level to the right). Original features include the oak panelling throughout, the oak-fronted bar counter and the Tudor-style stone-effect fireplace in the bar - but the bar back may be a reconstruction. A large rear extension houses the dining room.

Northamptonshire

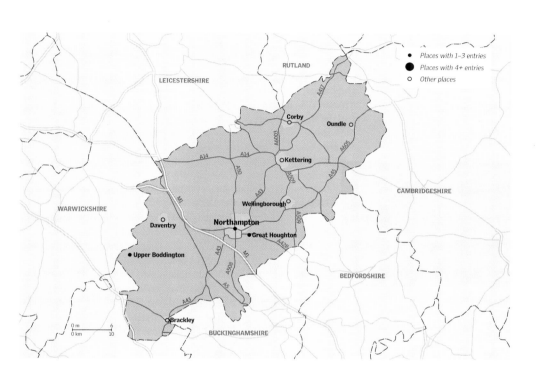

Places with 1–3 entries
Places with 4+ entries
Other places

Great Houghton

8 Cherry Tree Lane, NN4 7AT
01604 761399
Grade II listed
LPA: Northampton

The old snug, Old Cherry Tree

Old Cherry Tree

A 16th-century village pub, with thatch covering a corrugated iron roof, which expanded into an adjoining cottage in the late 1950s and has changed little since. The lounge bar, a long room on two levels, has late 1950s bar fittings including a coopered-effect counter front with brass straps for 'hoops'; a counter on the right has a half-timbered effect front whilst the bar-back fittings are also mostly late 1950s. The front door leads into a quarry-tiled passage created by a settle let into a

partition wall. Slightly opened up to the left is a tiny, partially panelled snug with good built-in seating, including the settle, supported to a beam with a blacksmith's stay. Service is from another coopered-effect bar counter. The room on the left was private quarters and became a pub room in the 1980s, as did the dining room at the back.

Northampton
12 Drapery, NN1 2HG
01604 636739
Grade II listed
LPA: Northampton

Shipman's

Refitted in late Victorian times, with some 1938 changes, the three-room layout here is still discernible. In the narrow bar, the counter and bar back are Victorian and the wall-panelling is from the 1930s. Around 1985 a food bar was incorporated into the counter at one end and the bar back here is modern. Note the two sets of spirit cocks on the bar back - CAMRA is only aware of four other such sets in the country. Some of the spirits which these dispensed were allegedly

distilled in the attic. The vats were removed in the 1980s. At the Drapery end, a small snug is now accessed by a wide opening but the original half-doors remain. A wide doorway on Drum Lane leads to what used to be the completely separate 'Barrel Bar' whose bar counter was disproportionately large. The bar fittings and a dumb waiter had to go when the Council insisted on installation of a gents' WC. The original entrance doors survive in Drum Lane, with a barrel above. This room has some 1930s features such as the fireplace, two niches and the small roof over the corner where the bar was situated. Until the 1980s, the pub only sold beer in half pints and even today the price list shows beer prices in halves. The pub has been closed but should have re-opened, hopefully unscathed, by the time this guide is published.

Upper Boddington
32 Warwick Road, NN11 6DH
01327 260364
Grade II listed
LPA: South Northamptonshire

Plough

The servery is an unusual feature in this early 18th-century stone-built, thatched pub. Outside doors labelled 'Public Bar' and 'Smoke Room' lead to a small room, with a floor part flagstoned and part quarry-tiled, betraying the fact that two rooms were combined in the 1980s. This was supposedly to make skittle-playing safer - cheeses were formerly thrown from the narrow passage into the public bar

making it necessary to stop play when anyone wanted to enter or leave the pub! The original servery/cellar is at the rear and installation of the bar counter has made the drinking area very tight. From the entrance lobby on two levels is a small lounge, formerly two tiny rooms, with a small modern counter and Raeburn cooker. The dining room occupies a modern extension.

Nottinghamshire

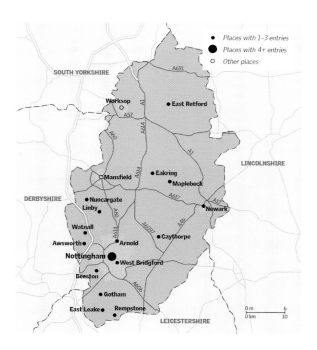

Places with 1–3 entries
Places with 4+ entries
Other places

SOUTH YORKSHIRE

Worksop

East Retford

LINCOLNSHIRE

Eakring
Maplebeck

Mansfield

DERBYSHIRE

Nuncargate
Linby

Newark

Watnall

Awsworth

Arnold

Caythorpe

Nottingham

West Bridgford

Beeston

Gotham

East Leake

Rempstone

LEICESTERSHIRE

0 m   6
0 km   10

Arnold

Oxclose Lane, NG5 6FZ
0115 926 5211
Grade II listed
LPA: Nottingham

Oxclose

A large estate pub of 1939, designed by Nottingham architect T. Cecil Howitt for Home Brewery. The external Tudor styling continues inside in the surviving doors and timber detailing. To the right of the entrance is a large plain bar with original counter and doors plus wooden surrounds to the servery. The former lounge-hall on the left has an alcove overlooking the garden. Also on this side of the building are a central front room with Tudor-style 'Smoke Room' lettering above the doorway and a rear lounge whose doors have been removed. All these left-hand rooms have original bar counters and surrounds and good ceilings, with vine decoration on the cornices. There are, though, several recent accretions like the lobby to the bar and some partitions plus unfortunate modern bar backs. The pub closed permanently just as this book was going to print.

Arnold, Daybrook
8-10 Mansfield Road, NG5 3GG
0115 926 8864
Grade II listed
LPA: Gedling

Vale Hotel ★

Like the Test Match Hotel across the Trent at West Bridgford, the splendid Art Deco interior here displays the kind of civilised 'improved public house' arrangements that inter-war clients, customers and licensing justices all thought desirable. This is another late 1930s design by T. Cecil Howitt for the local Home Brewery and it retains features like the rounded projections either side and metal windows. Much of the sleek, Art Deco interior also survives. To the left of the lovely glazed entrance lobby is the wonderful smoke room with original wall-panelling, counter and bar back, plus roundels bearing the Home Brewery initials - all this would be at home on a luxury trans-Atlantic liner. The direct entrance from the lobby was, though, blocked in 2011 with the doorway transferred to the far end to create a link to what was the public bar (where the counter and panelling are recent). On the right is a spacious lounge, entered through what is now a wide opening from the drinking lobby area. The back room (now a carvery) was added in period style in 1964.

The Art Deco-style smoke room at the Vale is one of Britain's classic pub rooms from the 1930s

Awsworth

Awsworth Lane, NG16 2RN
0115 932 9821
Unlisted
LPA: Ashfield

Gate

A Georgian-style, mid-Victorian building, though only the snug on the left survives from the original layout - it has old fixed benches but the fireplace has gone. Most of what we see dates from a 1950s remodelling which brought two living rooms at the back into pub use. One is the main bar with a 1950s counter and plain bar back and fixed seating of the same vintage. The other room serves as a lounge - all the fittings seem to be from the 1950s refit. The central entrance leads into a T-shaped hall with staircase to a function room. This area is a popular 'drinking passage' with a few tables and chairs and the servery straight ahead with a small Fifties-style hatch counter. The pool room is a recent creation in space previously occupied by toilets.

Beeston

20 Church Street, NG9 1FY
0115 925 4738
Grade II listed
LPA: Broxtowe

The flooring and woodwork in the public bar at the Crown probably date from around 1880

Crown

The star feature here is the original layout of four rooms, known as The Shambles, retained when this early 19th-century pub was greatly extended in 1976. The original, now subsidiary, door is in Middle Street and leads into a quarry-tiled passage. Through a pair of open doors is a sliding hatch and intact stable door with shelf and part-glazed upper door. The very small public bar on the right has a quarry-tiled floor and bar fittings dating from around 1880. The counter has a herringbone-panelled front and a bowed top of some age while the mirrored bar back contains four small cupboards. The furniture comprises an old bench and three small tables. Beyond another glazed partition wall is a tiny snug, formerly an off-sales. Back in the entrance passage, the snug on the left has old fixed seating on three sides. The Games Room is the last of this suite of old rooms and has vintage dado panelling and fixed seating of different dates. The curved bar counter could well have replaced a hatch in the inter-war era. Dating the panelling is made difficult by it being painted, but a long-standing customer insists that this portion is unchanged since his first visit back in 1937.

Beeston

85 Dovecote Lane, NG9 1JG
0115 925 4049
Unlisted
LPA: Broxtowe

Victoria Hotel

This large former hotel right by Beeston railway station was built by Ind Coope in 1899 and restored by its new owners, Tynemill, in 1994. You enter into a lobby with a former snug or off-sales straight ahead - now used for storage. On the right is a good plain bar, self-contained with its own toilets. In the main bar to the left the back corner has

been opened out to give access to two further rooms (mainly used for dining in the day). Doors, windows and benches look Victorian but there was clearly a makeover in the 1930s when the bar serveries (largely intact and with Art Deco features) were added to both main rooms - the dado panelling, floors and fireplaces are of the same era. In the rear lobby is a staircase with a fine stained glass window.

The middle bar, Victoria Hotel

Caythorpe

29 Main St, NG14 7ED
0115 966 3520
Unlisted
LPA: Newark & Sherwood

Black Horse

A very traditional early 18th-century cottage pub which has seen some modernisation but whose two-room layout is largely intact. Beyond the front lobby (a recent addition) the main bar is on the right. The lapped timber counter and benches are at least forty years old though the brick fireplace is new. A small snug is on the left. Instead of a counter it has just a small part of the bar back on which drinks are placed when poured. The wall bench seating is old but, again, the fireplace is a let down. Both rooms had separate entrances before the lobby was built. Home of Caythorpe Brewery.

Eakring

Bilsthorpe Road, NG22 0DG
01623 870264
Unlisted
LPA: Newark & Sherwood

Savile Arms

An early 17th-century brick-built corner pub with a lovely exterior. The porch entrance on the main road is out of use so you go in at the corner facing the car park. This entrance opens out into a central bar-lobby where the servery and bar back are quite modern but traditional in style. To the rear right, the lounge has a real fire and service through a hatch-counter but no fixed seating. A corridor on the left leads to the unused front door. In the corner is a small tap room with benches and hatch service while on the other side can be found a tiny snug-lobby and then a pool room with red-tiled floors. Note the numbers on all doors.

East Leake

1 Brookside, LE12 6PB

01509 856658

Unlisted

LPA: Rushcliffe

Three Horseshoes

Built by Home Brewery in 1963-4 behind the original pub: the latter was then demolished and the front patio and car park now occupy its footprint. Above the front door is a blacksmith's scene in deep relief, which replaced the original bronze version. You enter a wide lobby then a large public bar with a distinctive period counter front and bar back of the same era (with fridges replacing part of the lower shelves). Some, but not all of, the fixed seating survives. Doors at the end of the lobby lead to a small room centre-left known by locals as the 'Penny Lounge' (because beer here was once dearer by that amount). This room has interesting panelling and counter fronts. The rear lounge was even more expensive - by tuppence - when the pub opened. It has the same style panelling and counters plus a Tudor-style fireplace but the bar back has undergone some tampering. Note the coat hooks along the counter front.

East Retford

39 Grove Street, DN22 6LA

01777 702742

Unlisted

LPA: Bassetlaw

Turks Head

This 1936 rebuild, with 'Brewers' Tudor' first floor and coaching arch on the left, retains many original fittings but its three rooms and off-sales have been knocked together. The walls throughout the pub have oak fielded panelling to picture-frame height and at the front are two

original fireplaces - note the Turk's head symbols on the copper canopies. The counter is original, with more fielded panelling, as is the bar back but the servery may have been adroitly altered to serve the joined-up front rooms. The rear area now acts as a pool room with parquet floor, more original fixed seating and service bells above the fireplace. The rare pub game of ring the bull is played here.

1930s fittings at the Turks Head

Gotham

Leake Road, NG11 0JL

0115 983 0306

Unlisted

LPA: Rushcliffe

Cuckoo Bush

An 1858 building with an unusual layout. The main entrance leads to a drinkers' lobby, then a smoke room on the left - the modern fittings here suggest it is a recent addition. On the right is a wonderful, largely unaltered bar with old narrow benches, old counter (but new top and bar back), wood-surround fireplace and cast-iron tables. A narrow passage takes you to a large rear lounge which is an amalgamation of two small rooms. The counter is genuinely old but not so the other fittings.

Linby
Main Street, NG15 8AE
0115 963 3334
Unlisted
LPA: Gedling

Horse & Groom

An old (possibly 17th century) pub extended by Home Brewery in the 1920s and again in 1937 - the multi-room layout dates from those last alterations. Entering the lobby, you originally faced the off-sales but this has now been absorbed into the right-hand lounge. That room still has its 1930s panelling and wood surround to the fireplace but the bar counter is 1960s work and the bar back even newer. Back in the lobby, the left-hand door takes you into a parquet-floored passage with panelled walls; it is separated from a small snug by a rare part-glazed partition wall. The snug has much from the 1930s - the counter, fireplace, wall-panelling and some of the bar back. The left-hand lounge has seen a good deal of refurbishment with only the parquet floor surviving from 1937. Another passageway leads from the lounge back door to the original entrance door. The larger bar-lounge, rear right, was added in 1937 and has a large inglenook fireplace, original slatted benches and bar counter plus a bar back mixing old with new.

The snug, Horse & Groom

Maplebeck
Main Street, NG22 0BS
01636 636306
Unlisted
LPA: Newark & Sherwood

Beehive

Supposedly the county's smallest pub, the Beehive was built in 1803 and occupies a delightful setting on a bank above the road. Rooms are on each side of the central entrance with a small bar on the right and tiny snug with hatch counter to the left. The simple decor, beamed ceilings, simple benches, and a copper-topped counter, dates mainly from the 1950s or 1960s though the fireplaces are more recent.

Newark
38 George Street, NG24 1LU
01636 707294
Unlisted
LPA: Newark & Sherwood

Newcastle Arms

Most of what you see here is the result of a late-1950s refit, though the building dates from 1842 (and was altered significantly in the 1930s). A passage from the main door retains its off-sales hatch. The lounge, on the right, has a lapped bar counter, modest bar back, fixed seating and Formica-topped tables. In the public bar on the left you'll find a lino-tiled floor, typical Formica-topped 1950s bar counter, another modest bar back, fixed seating and ply panel dado. Another feature redolent of the period is the sliding door to the servery in the rear passage behind the bars.

Newark

117 Barnby Gate, NG24 1QZ
01636 704333
Unlisted
LPA: Newark & Sherwood

Roaring Meg

A Victorian pub, last refurbished around 1960. Before this, the L-shaped public bar consisted of two rooms - original benches line the outside walls but the counter and bar back are from the refit. In the large lobby, with its dado of green-glazed bricks, you can still see the off-sales hatch. Another *c*.1960 counter, this time in the classic curved style of the time, dominates the rear bar. This was the Vine until local brewery Springhead bought it in 2013.

Nottingham, Bulwell

St Albans Road, NG6 9JS
0115 927 8542
Unlisted
LPA: Nottingham

Newstead Abbey

A splendid large early 20th-century brick-built pub with a corner tower. Inside there has been some opening out but the original and unusual layout is easy to discern. This features a large plain bar on the left, an island servery with a wide drinking corridor behind and, front-right, an opened-out snug with unused bell-pushes.

Nottingham, City Centre

1 Brewhouse Yard, Castle Road, NG1 6AD
0115 947 3171
Grade II listed
LPA: Nottingham

The Ward Room is one of several at the Olde Trip to be carved out of the solid rock beneath Nottingham Castle

Olde Trip to Jerusalem ★

Parts of this remarkable building are 17th century - but not from the 12th as the made-up date outside would have us believe! Its uniqueness derives from a series of rooms carved out of the soft sandstone of Castle Rock. Alterations in 1997-8 did not impact adversely on the historic core and, indeed, won a CAMRA/English Heritage design award. A flagstone passage leads to the Ward Room (named after the family of licensees from 1894 to 1989), hollowed out of the rock. Opposite, the servery is of varied but fairly indeterminate dates. The tiny rock-cut snug beyond was created during the alterations. Up a staircase is 'Mortimer's Room', a cavernous lounge refitted about 1930 with a quarter-circle counter and brick fireplace: beware the 'cursed galleon', not cleaned for over 50 years after the mysterious deaths of the last three people who tried to do just that! From here, a passage (again from 1997-8) leads to another small room, previously an office. Back downstairs, room no.3 may once have been a kitchen and is known as Yorkey's Room after 'Yorkey' Ward, landlord 1894-1914 (see his inn sign on the wall). The adjacent snug was converted from living accommodation in 1996.

Nottingham, City Centre
11 Mansfield Road, NG1 3FB
0115 947 2152
Grade II listed
LPA: Nottingham

Peacock

A very rare opportunity to experience something once common in pubs - table service. Sit on the bench seating in the right-hand lounge, press one of the numerous bell-pushes set in brass-plates and a member of staff will come and take your order (except on Friday or Saturday nights) (see p.28). The lounge itself is little altered since a 1930s refit and has carved bench seating throughout with turned legs and moulded arms plus a wooden-studded frieze above and the odd baffle. Non-table service is from a hatch/doorway at the back of the bar. The good-quality fittings in the public bar date only from 1993. What looks like an old glazed publican's office can be spied towards the back of the bar servery - only about a dozen of these survive countrywide.

Nottingham, City Centre
St Nicholas Street, NG1 6AJ
0115 958 9432
Grade II listed
LPA: Nottingham

Salutation

The present pub is a combination of three buildings, the oldest of which has a 1240 date outside but is more likely to be a mix of 16th- and mid-18th-century structures. The King Charles snug right of the narrow, flagged entrance passage is the oldest room, with genuinely ancient beams but fittings from the Thirties and Sixties. Left of the passage is an extension into an adjoining 19th-century building and the small, bare-boarded Cromwell Snug again features a mix of Thirties and Sixties work. The passage then widens into a lobby area with bench seating and a door to extensive cellars hewn from the sandstone (to which access might be possible at quiet times). At the end is the third building, a Tudor-style hall from the 1930s with a much-altered interior, including a later first-floor gallery.

Nottingham, Sherwood
Edwards Lane, NG5 3HU
0115 926 5612
Grade II listed
LPA: Nottingham

Five Ways ★

A prominent 'Brewers' Tudor' roadhouse of 1936-7, for Newark brewers Warwicks & Richardsons to designs by local architect A.E. Eberlin and which recently avoided destructive planned changes thanks to local campaigning. The layout, intact except for a lost off-sales, ranges round an L-shaped corridor which has sashed screens to the servery and a disused telephone booth. At the front are a corner bar and, on the left, a smoke room (now called the 'Ken Yarwood Room') with fine panelling, Tudor fireplace and formerly sashed screen to a narrow servery. On the other side of the corridor are a large lounge with

1930s woodwork and counter screens at the Five Ways

decoratively-banded segmental plaster ceiling, and a long function room which now serves as the main bar. This shift of focus leaves the rest of the pub somewhat isolated and this is matched by a generally cheap and modern furnishing scheme. Closed as of February 2015 - future uncertain.

Nottingham, Sneinton
Sneinton Dale, NG2 4HJ
Ex-directory
Unlisted
LPA: Nottingham

Dale

Both entrances to this 1930s Shipstone's pub have original doors and mosaic floors sporting Art Deco designs. The front entrance takes you into a plain bar with benches but no fireplace. The corner entrance leads to the lounge which was once two rooms. The bench seating with bell-pushes at the front is original but that at the back is from the 1960s, when a fireplace was lost. Both rooms have original counters, with modern tops, and plain shelving and bar backs, the latter with minimal Art Deco detailing. A terrazzo-floored L-shaped corridor at the rear links the rooms.

Nottingham, Sneinton
Lord Nelson Street, NG2 4AG
0115 911 0069
Grade II listed
LPA: Nottingham

Lord Nelson

Originally farm cottages, this delightful building long predates the surrounding development. A passage from the garden leads to the main bar, small and square, with servery behind. Through an arch on the left is a snug whilst at the rear left is a snug bar with a small counter and separate street entrance. Finally comes a plain room on the right. Most fittings are from a refurbishment in the 1950s.

The public bar,
Lord Nelson

Nottingham, Sneinton
248 Carlton Road, NG3 2NB
0115 950 4328
Unlisted
LPA: Nottingham

March Hare

The only significant change to this pub since it was built for Warwicks & Richardsons of Newark in 1958, is the absorbtion of the off-sales into the smoke room in the 1960s. All the bar fittings, fixed seating, toilets and even the furniture date from 1958, their longevity no doubt connected to the fact that the same tenant (George Dove)

was in charge from opening until his recent death (and his widow still runs the pub). Even the till is dated 1959, having been converted to decimal in 1971. The weighing machine in the lobby still records pounds and stones - none of your foreign kilos here! Please note the pub keeps traditional hours, closing in the afternoon.

Intact pub rooms from the 1950s, like the public bar at the March Hare, are now very rare indeed

Nottingham, Wollaton Village
Wollaton Road, NG8 2AF
0115 928 6970
Unlisted
LPA: Nottingham

Admiral Rodney

A good number of early 20th-century fittings survive in this 18th-century pub, re-fronted and hugely extended by Home Brewery in 1924. The original part consists of the three rooms at the front-right which were refurbished in the 1950s. The extension is of classic inter-war brick design and the panelling, counter and fireplace are from 1924. All this is overlaid with much more recent work.

Nottingham
282 - 284 Arkwright Street,
Trent Bridge, NG2 2GR
0115 986 4502
Unlisted
LPA: Nottingham

Embankment

Formerly the Boots Social Club, this early 20th century, Tudor-style building of 1903 by architect Alfred Nelson Bromley, reopened as a pub and conference centre in 2010. The main bar, in a baronial-style hall, is lit by an ornamented skylight and has a fine staircase. The old bar counter retains shutters and the bar back could be of similar vintage. At the rear is a glazed screen with twin doors leading to a fully-equipped snooker room. A hatch to the side of the bar has another old shutter though the counter front looks to be of the 1970s. The lounge occupies what used to be a retail branch of Boots. Upstairs, the splendid Committee Room has a wood-block floor, panelled walls, an inglenook fireplace and other period features. The fine stained glass was designed by the well-known architect Morley Horder. Elsewhere are a ballroom and, in the basement, a well-used skittle alley and a further, more recent, bar.

Nuncargate

Nuncargate Road, NG17 9EH
Ex-directory
Unlisted
LPA: Ashfield

Cricketers Arms

Most of what you see here dates from a 1950s Home Brewery refurbishment of what had been two distinct Victorian buildings. The lounge has its original copper-topped counter but was extended eastwards in the 1970s to create two seating bays and most fittings are from that time. The bar is more authentically a product of the austere Fifties - counter with a Formica top, simple bar back and fixed seating and period fireplace. The adjacent cricket ground is where the legendary Harold Larwood first played, hence the memorabilia inside the pub.

Rempstone

Main Street, LE12 6RH
01509 880669
Unlisted
LPA: Rushcliffe

Closed weekday lunchtimes except Tuesdays

White Lion

This small, traditional cottage-style village inn was probably built in the 19th century and refurbished in the late 1950s/early 1960s, since when little has changed. Two tiny rooms - a public bar on the left and snug on the right - were combined and the then-new fittings included the brick fireplaces, plain benches all round, bar counter, simple bar shelves and tiled floor. The originally outside toilets are linked to the pub by an extension which houses a pool table.

Watnall

Main Road, NG16 1HT
0115 938 6774
Unlisted
LPA: Broxtowe

Queens Head

The pub has evolved from a small, partitioned, basic tap room on the right, now opened up to the passageway - a section of partition was removed in the early 1990s and the 1930s fireplace replaced. The servery is a mixture of old and new, the glazed area at the top definitely being the former. A short passage leads to a small snug-type room with 1930s tiled fireplace and fixed seating - the room was supposedly in use in 1906. The large lounge occupies what was once a row of back-to-back cottages.

The Queens Head contains work of various periods: the servery shown here is a mixture of the old and new

61

Test Match Hotel

West Bridgford

Gordon Square, Gordon Road,
NG2 5LP

0115 981 1481

Grade II* listed

LPA: Rushcliffe

In the Test Match and the Vale Hotel, Arnold (p.52), Nottinghamshire has two of the best Art Deco pub interiors in England. It was built in 1938 to the designs of A.C.Wheeler for brewers Hardys & Hansons of Kimberley. The pub name derives from the nearby Trent Bridge cricket ground. A revolving door sweeps you into a glorious two-storey, ash-panelled lounge with ceiling lighting reminiscent of a great inter-war cinema. The (later) wall paintings by local artist T.L.B. Hutchinson have a cricketing theme. To the right is the former gents-only smoke room with a striking arched approach to the toilets (obviously no provision for ladies): as elsewhere, they are as built. A wide staircase from the lounge leads up to the beautifully preserved Boundary Bar, originally a cocktail lounge, with its semi-circular counter. During a major but sensitive refurbishment in 2001 the lounge was linked to what was an assembly room at the back. A side entrance takes you into the remarkable public bar, complete with its jazzy terrazzo floor, tiered counter and angular slate fireplaces.

The public bar is a remarkable survival from the late 1930s with its banded counter and jazzy terrazzo floor

Shropshire

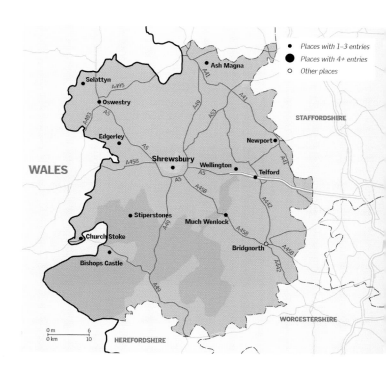

- ● Places with 1–3 entries
- ● Places with 4+ entries
- ○ Other places

WALES

STAFFORDSHIRE

WORCESTERSHIRE

HEREFORDSHIRE

0 m 6
0 km 10

Ash Magna
SY13 4DR
01948 663153
Unlisted
LPA: Shropshire

Closed weekday lunchtimes

White Lion

Enthusiasts of 1930s decor will find much to enjoy in the lounge bar of this village pub. The unusual bar counter features rustic vertical panels and the bar-back fitting has a curved Art Deco-style top (partly removed so staff can walk between the serveries). There is more Art Deco in the fireplace's wood surround while some tables and chairs are in the 'publican's rustic' mode popular at the time. The public bar has a long counter with panels from around 1960 between older pilasters and with a recent bar top. Also dating from the 1960s are changes to the bar back and the brick fireplace but the bench seating in the rear narrow part is old and the beamed ceiling older still. The inner lobby retains a two-part off-sales window.

Bishops Castle

Market Square, SY9 5BN

01588 638403

Grade II listed

LPA: Shropshire

Castle Hotel

An 18th-century hotel, notable for the splendidly cosy bar to the left of the main entrance. The fittings here are mainly late 19th/early 20th century. Above the boarded dado is imitation boarding, a cheap substitute for the real thing often used at the time. The counter has a simple, match-boarded front while the bar back comprises old shelving on a mirrored backing. A glazed screen is on the right and plain brick fireplace to the left. The lounge and panelled dining room are largely devoid of old fittings and the bar rear left is all modern.

Church Stoke

SY15 6SP

01588 620231

Unlisted

LPA: Shropshire

Blue Bell

The public bar here was refitted in 1949 since when nothing much has changed. It has a quarry-tiled floor, Formica-topped bar counter, plain bar-back shelves, brick fireplace and bare oak seating. The front

lobby also dates from 1949, the bar door being the original front door. The lounge was converted from a stable in the 1960s from when most of the fittings can be dated - lapped bar counter, glass shelves on the wooden bar back, leatherette bench seating, chairs and Formica-topped tables. The same family has owned the pub since 1926.

The public bar is much as it was when refitted back in 1949

Edgerley

SY10 8ES

01743 741242

Unlisted

LPA: Shropshire

Closed lunchtimes Monday-Thursday

Royal Hill

This pub, with its fine views, was built in 1777 according to its date-stone, though the brickwork suggests a 19th-century refronting. The original rooms are the front bar, created by two high-backed settles to form a passage from the door, and the tiny rear servery with a Victorian counter. The lounge on the left and room on the right are converts from private accommodation; the former recently lost its

'front room' style with the introduction of modern furniture. Another change, in the bar, has seen a short passage created to access the right-hand room. Two further rooms to the left of the lounge were sculpted out of former stables. Hatch service to two rooms.

Simple fittings characterise the bar at the Royal Hill

Much Wenlock

High Street, TF13 6AQ

01952 727212

Grade II* listed

LPA: Shropshire

Gaskell Arms Hotel

Built in the Regency period, the hotel sits on the stone foundations of the erstwhile Rindleford Hall. William Butler & Co. of Wolverhampton carried out a full renovation after buying it in 1960 and the bar fittings survive virtually unchanged. The small back public bar has an old painted dado, wood-panel counter with metal studs and inlaid Formica top, old bar back with glass shelving and a carved wood fireplace - but some fixed seating has recently been lost. The front lounge is in two parts each side of a back-to-back fireplace, the left-hand section having a distinctive counter and a bar back similar to that in the public bar. A split door in the passage between the bars bears the words 'Garden Service', being opposite a tiled passage to the garden. The quarter-circle counter opposite the car park entrance now serves as the reception desk. A dining room front left is served from a hatch.

Newport

2 Stafford Road, TF10 7LX

07796 33665

Unlisted

LPA: Telford & Wrekin

Opens 2pm Monday-Thursday

New Inn

A three-roomed pub which has seen few changes in the last forty years. The public bar on the left was once two rooms; the old centrally-placed bar counter has a 1960s red Formica top plus black-painted tiles on the front and a small hatch-like opening above. On the passage side of the servery is an attractive part-glazed partition wall with bar-back shelving attached. The front-right room was opened up to the passage in the 1990s - it has an inglenook-style 1930s fireplace, seating at least forty years old and a good 'Vaults' etched window. The seating in the rear right room is of a similar vintage. Outside toilets across the Staffordshire blue-brick yard.

Oswestry

17 Church Street, SY11 2SZ

01691 659254

Grade II listed

LPA: Shropshire

Oak

Most of what you see today in this early 19th-century pub is from a 1950s refurbishment. The small public bar, accessed from a porch, front-right, has a slatted wooden counter and period bar-back fittings, 1950s fireplace within an older inglenook and fixed seating. Back outside, a door in the left-hand wall labelled 'Gents Bar' on the passage side takes you into a quarry-tiled corridor with a partition to the servery and an off-sales hatch still with sliding door. The door at the end of this passage opens into the lounge, somewhat expanded in recent times - an advert on the wall shows the previous smaller version. More 1950s features here - another slatted wood counter, same bar-back fittings, brick fireplace and fixed seating. Note the sign 'Wrexham Lager Sold "On Draught" and Off the Ice'.

Selattyn

Glyn Road, SY10 7DN
01691 650247
Unlisted
LPA: Shropshire

Closed Monday-Tuesday
and lunchtimes
Wednesday-Saturday

The simply
appointed
Victorian public
bar forms the core
of the Cross Keys

Cross Keys

A modest four-roomed village pub which, until 1994, doubled as the village shop, hence the big window on the right. The delightful small bar on the right of the passageway is the old core of the pub; it has mostly Victorian or early 20th-century fittings (but a later fireplace) and red and black quarry-tiled flooring. Across the corridor is the

'Music Room' which hosts Irish music every Thursday - its inglenook fireplace may date from the 1930s. Further back, another two rooms have come into pub use fairly recently. One, formerly a living room, serves as a games room and the only old fittings are the wall cupboards. The other is a large function room in the former stables.

Shrewsbury

1 Church Street, SY1 1UG
01743 362398
Grade II listed
LPA: Shropshire

Loggerheads ★

Occupying an 18th-century building in the old heart of the town, this wonderfully unspoilt pub still has four separate rooms. Off the left-hand passageway are a serving hatch and the former 'Gents Only' bar - now an outlawed feature of pub life (see p.35). The latter is formed by a timber and glass partition which doubles as a high-back settle and with an outside wall lined with recycled 16th- or 17th-century

oak panelling. Some old (non-working) bell-pushes and a traditional slate shove ha'penny board complete the scene. The tiny front bar in the centre is a homely space with plain furnishings. Also miniscule is the snug (the 'Poet's Room') at the rear left with its old padded bench seating. The corridor runs round the back of the servery to the parquet-floored lounge bar which occupies a (probably) inter-war extension; it has fixed seating on two sides, a brick fireplace and service from a hatch to the side of the servery.

The former 'Gents Only' bar has much old woodwork

Shrewsbury

32 Coton Hill, SY1 2DZ
01743 351007
Unlisted
LPA: Shropshire

Opens 4pm
weekdays

Woodman

A brick and half-timbered pub, rebuilt in 1925, with the two shop windows around the jug & bottle door added in the 1960s. In the bar, the counter has attractive fielded panelling and the fixed seating and tiled floor are also original (but not so the bar top and fireplace). The

lounge, once two small rooms, has inter-war panelled walls and the bar back could well be original. The brick and Formica-topped bar counter, though, is a 1960s insertion and the fireplaces have modern surrounds.

The fittings survive from the rebuilding of the pub in 1925

Stiperstones

SY5 0LZ
01743 791327
Unlisted
LPA: Shropshire

Stiperstones Inn

A pub since 1840, the Stiperstones has been in the same family for 45 years and has changed little since a late 1950s refit. The lobby retains its off-sales hatch in a glazed screen then, on the left, is the lounge which is fully panelled in typical 1950s style. The counter appears to be from the same era, as do the fireplace and fixed seating, but the bar back could be somewhat later - the mirror mosaic in the fittings was popular in the 1960s. More 1950s work in the public bar (curved counter, plain bar back, brick fireplace and fixed seating) though the exposed brick dado seems to be of a later date. The two dining rooms at the back have a few old fittings. Out-buildings have been converted into a well-stocked village shop.

Telford, Madeley

Blist's Hill Museum, TF7 5DP
01952 433424
Unlisted
LPA: Telford & Wrekin

New Inn

The New Inn was moved to the museum from the corner of Green Lane and Hospital Street, Birchills, Walsall, in 1981-2. Small street-corner local pubs like this once existed in their thousands but intact examples have now all but disappeared. The public bar and tap room are both very simply appointed with plain wooden panelling, bare benches and cast-iron tables. The furnishings in the more 'respectable' parlour at the back are only slightly less uncomplicated. Beer prices, however, are distinctly up-to-date. Admission charge to the Museum.

Telford, Wrockwardine Wood

Plough Road, TF2 7AW
No landline
Grade II listed
LPA: Telford & Wrekin

Bulls Head ★

This pub, with its thrilling and colourful display of tiles and glazed bricks, dates from around 1904. The ceramics are by Maw & Co. of Jackfield (in the nearby Ironbridge Gorge) who were perhaps the world's largest manufacturer of decorative tiles at that time. The frontage has bands of green and yellow glazed brick on the upper floors with strips of mosaic below. In the front room, the tiling extends from floor-to-ceiling in various designs and colours. The floor too is tiled in patterns of brown, buff, blue and white. The counter (with unusual strips of low-relief carved decoration) and the bar back are also Edwardian. Some of the window glass is original,

including that on the first floor and the door glass inscribed 'Bar'. However, you will need to ask the bar staff for access to this room as it is rarely open at present. There was formerly a corridor from the right-hand doorway to the rear and the rear- and left-hand parts were created in 1984.

1904 tiling and woodwork

Wellington

148a Holyhead Road, TF1 2DL
01952 244954
Grade II listed
LPA: Telford & Wrekin

Opens 4pm Monday-Wednesday

Cock Hotel

This 18th-century coaching inn on Watling Street saw a good deal of refurbishment in the mid-20th century. From the lobby, with its wood-panelled walls, you enter a panelled reception area with an open staircase. The bar on the right (now focused on Belgian beers) has upholstered fixed seating, a panelled and leatherette-cushioned counter with copper top and a period bar back, much of which looks to date from the 1960s. A wood-panelled lounge further back has square panelling with bell-pushes and a fine brick fireplace - all 1950s work. The main bar ('The Old Wrekin Tap') has a 1950s counter, upholstered benches, half-height-panelling and a modern fireplace.

Staffordshire

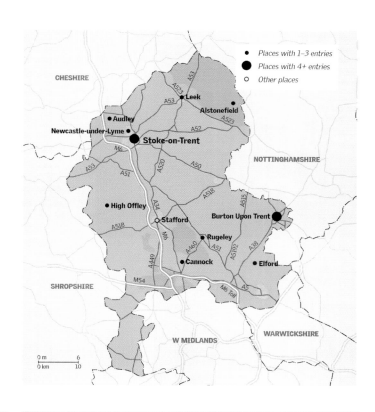

Map legend:
- Places with 1–3 entries
- Places with 4+ entries
- Other places

CHESHIRE

Leek
Alstonefield
Audley
Newcastle-under-Lyme
Stoke-on-Trent

NOTTINGHAMSHIRE

High Offley
Stafford
Burton Upon Trent
Rugeley
Cannock
Elford

SHROPSHIRE

W MIDLANDS
WARWICKSHIRE

0 m — 6
0 km — 10

Alstonefield
DE6 2FX
01335 310205
Unlisted
LPA: Staffordshire Moorlands

George

A rare example of an interior refitted in the 1960s and where some parts have hardly changed since. In the public bar, the counter, bar back, fixed seating and stone fireplace all date from that particular era - the counter especially, with casks embedded in the stonework and copper top, is typical of the time. A gap leads to a second area with more 1960s seating. The dining room on the left was revamped in 2006 at which time the fine stone fireplace, previously covered by plasterboard, was re-exposed. Just past the door to the bar is the former off-sales.

Audley

18 Church Street, ST7 8DE
01782 720486
Unlisted
LPA: Newcastle-Under-Lyme

The lounge

Butchers Arms ★

This attractive brick-and-half-timbered pub is much the same today as when rebuilt in 1933. The entrance leads to a spacious corridor with panelling and quarry-tiled flooring, the latter continuing into the small public bar on the right. This has an impressive ceiling, divided into three deep compartments and with rich cornices bearing grapes and Tudor roses. The counter is original, albeit with a new top.

Further back, the larger lounge also has a triple-compartmented ceiling and a similar frieze. Also on show are a Tudor-style fireplace (with heraldic crest above), good dado panelling and a counter ornamented with fleur-de-lys (but again a new top). Rear left is the smoke room, still with original fireplace, fixed seating and bell-pushes; here the rather simpler ceiling has a border with oak leaves. In the large upstairs function room, only the fireplace is from 1933. The pub was built with an early form of electric-powered air conditioning and the vents can still be seen in the public rooms. The only major loss is the off-sales on the right side.

Burton upon Trent

43 Cross Street, DE14 1EG
01283 523551
Unlisted
LPA: East Staffordshire

The Coopers Tavern is one of little more than a dozen pubs which have no bar counter (see Index, No counter pubs). In the main room customers and the drinks are in unusual proximity

Coopers Tavern ★

This remarkable pub is famous not only for being the former Bass brewery tap but also for having no real bar counter. It began life as an overflow store for special malts for the brewery and by 1826 was the repository for Bass's Imperial Stout, after which senior members of the brewery began using it as their private pub. Licensing as a public house followed in 1858 but the back area remained the fiefdom of the select few until about 1950, the *hoi polloi* being served at a hatch

between this 'cellar' and the passage beyond. Now anyone can drink there, perching on three benches or in a raised area in the corner; within the same space a large variety of beers and other drinks are stored, creating a drinking environment like no other. A large lounge occupies the front of the building, and the two types of quarry tiles suggest this may once have been two separate rooms; it has old benches and the bell-pushes still work. The snug (front left) is a recent creation sculpted out of private quarters.

Burton upon Trent
17 Derby Road, DE14 1RU
01283 543674
Unlisted
LPA: East Staffordshire

Derby Inn

A Victorian terrace pub, cherishable for its largely intact 1960s refit. From the tiny entrance lobby, still with off-sales hatch, a door on the right leads into the narrow, lino-floored public bar. Thousands of pubs in the 1960s had bar fittings similar to those here - counter with Formica top (but new front) and bar back made up from simple shelving, some with Formica tops and some of glass. There is early 20th-century seating in the bay window and on the right-hand side - the latter still with its maker's label. The room has recently been knocked through at its far end to create more space. Back to the lobby, the door on the left leads into a small lounge with ply-panelling on the walls to three-quarter height. Both the bar counter and two sets of fixed seating are from the 1960s refit. Sadly, the juke-box of the same era longer functions.

Burton upon Trent
27 Victoria Street, DE14 2LP
01283 619716
Unlisted
LPA: East Staffordshire

Duke of York

The public bar here sports an attractively panelled Victorian bar counter with original top and bar-back shelves. Also of note are the boarded ceiling, the etched and frosted 'Vaults' windows and the leaded lights. The only recent change is the removal of a partition which separated out the tiny outdoor or 'horse box' on the left - see the markings on the ceiling. The rear lounge, formerly two rooms, has been much modernised with just a single etched window from past times.

Burton upon Trent
123 Calais Road, DE13 0UN
01283 543674
Unlisted
LPA: East Staffordshire

Wyggeston Hotel

A Salt's brewery pub of 1904, this has a little altered public bar with original bar counter and bar back, the latter featuring a large semi-circular mirror as well as cupboards, drawers and mirrored panels. The excellent vestibule entrance is no longer used. To the left a small 'Men Only' room has been modernised but some bar fittings remain. The large lounge on two levels is a 1984 opening out of a passageway with several rooms off it - two original fireplaces survive.

Cannock

35 St Johns Road, WS11 0AL
01543 574812
Grade II listed
LPA: Cannock Chase

Crystal Fountain ★

This plain, neo-Georgian pub of 1937 retains its original four-room layout and Moderne-style fittings. The only significant changes are the opening of a link between the public bar and the snug and the addition of a small counter in the lounge. The latter is to the rear left and to its right is a function room (formerly the 'non-smoking dining room') with large windows opening to the garden. Many period features survive, notably the bar counter and bar back, bench seating, sleek doors and the fitting out of the toilets on the left. The right-hand gents' is out of use and there never was a ladies' as the public bar was very much a male preserve. After a long period of decline, the pub was very carefully refurbished by Black Country Ales and reopened in May 2012.

The public bar and its 1930s servery

Elford

The Square, B79 9DB
01827 383602
Grade II listed
LPA: Lichfield

Crown

A charming, tucked-away, brick-built (mainly 18th-century) pub. On the right, a small public bar retains its Victorian bar back and counter plus old bench seating. The bar on the left suffered alterations in the 1950s but old panelling survives. The small room further left contains what may be an old cell - there was once a courtroom upstairs. It also has half-height panelling, parquet flooring and a 1950s fireplace. There have been various extensions and incorporations at the back, including the vaulted Old Cellar.

High Offley

Peggs Lane, Old Lea, ST20 0NG
01785 284569
Unlisted
LPA: Stafford

Anchor ★

Perhaps the most unspoilt example of a canal-side pub, with the front door facing the water rather than the road. It was built around 1830 to serve the Shropshire Union, England's last trunk narrow canal. The right-hand room is especially memorable, with its quarry-tiled floor, two high-backed settles, window bench and scrubbed tables - the ensemble creating a truly timeless atmosphere. The bar counter is decorated to resemble a narrow boat. The left-hand room was refitted in the early 1960s and reflects the tastes of that time. The pub has been in the same family since 1903. It is also one of only a handful where real ale can be fetched from the cellar and served from a jug.

The right-hand room has a fine pair of high-backed settles

Leek
17 Market Place, ST13 5HJ
01538 382918
Grade II listed
LPA: Staffordshire Moorlands

Bird in Hand

An impressive, market-place pub rebuilt in 1889 by local architects William Sugden & Son, also responsible for Leek's Nicholson Institute. To the left of the porch, with its mosaic floor, is the public bar with splendid carved and mirrored bar back and carved oak counter (with new top). On the right, the lounge has been combined with the lobby area around the modern counter but the fixed seating in the bay window and delicate wall-panelling are original. Rear-right, a small snug is used mainly for darts. A number of coloured and leaded windows add further interest to the interior.

Newcastle-under-Lyme, May Bank
Alexander Road, ST5 9PL
01782 619169
Unlisted
LPA: Newcastle-under-Lyme

Opens 3pm Monday-Thursday

Cricketers Arms

Although an old pub, the interest here derives mainly from a rebuild in 1935 following a fire. The central entrance leads into a terrazzo-tiled lobby, with a tiled dado and modern hatch counter. Beyond, the public bar may have been two rooms before the 1935 changes and most of the fittings are from that time (though the counter has a new top and tiled front). Front-right, a separate snug, now used for pool, has old benches and good ceiling cornice detail. The best room, though, is the splendid narrow lounge at the rear right. There are benches all round, except where a 'cocktail bar' was inserted in the 1950s, and above the benches is superb panelling with a few bell-pushes. Good ceiling cornices again. All the internal doors are from the 1935 refit.

Rugeley
19 Market Street, WS15 2JH
01889 586848
Grade II listed
LPA: Cannock Chase

Red Lion ★

Last refitted in the inter-war years, this popular three-room drinkers' pub occupies a 16th-century timber-framed building. The small public bar in the centre has some very old re-used panelling, a red quarry-tiled floor and a beamed ceiling. The fireplace was modified in the 1970s when the typical Banks's metal inset was installed (as it was in the other two rooms). The tiny cupboard left of the fireplace kept dry valuable items like salt. The counter seems to be inter-war while the bar back with turned shafts looks earlier. To the left, a snug has modern fittings but an inter-war fireplace. The games room on the right has panelling, old bench seating and a modern tiled floor.

The public bar, part of the inter-war refitting at the Red Lion

Stoke-on-Trent, Bucknall
248 Werrington Road,
ST2 9AW
01782 911843
Unlisted
LPA: Stoke-on-Trent

Travellers Rest

A 1930s build with four little-altered rooms. The lobby has a tiled dado on one side and the off-sales is still extant, albeit with a window replacing the hatch. The public bar has its original fixed seating and counter but the bar back is partly modernised. The narrow, so-called 'Chapel of Rest' is the most distinctive room with its original wall-panelling (with bell-pushes), counter and bar back - pity the replacement repro fireplace echoes the wrong period. The lobby bar at the back has a dado of fielded panelling and the old counter whilst the music room contains nothing of note (so to speak).

Stoke-on-Trent, Burslem
2 St John's Square, ST6 3AJ
07815 814809
Unlisted
LPA: Stoke-on-Trent

The public bar

Duke William

A prominent and largely intact pub from the 1930s. From the inner lobby, with its terrazzo floors, one door leads to an off-sales created by full-height glazed partition walls and a removed panel gives access to the public bar (the original door to this now being locked out of use). Another set of doors brings you to the lobby bar, also with a terrazzo floor and whose servery is surrounded by glazed screen-work up to the ceiling, with just the lower raising panels missing. Two

rooms lead off the corridor - there has been some opening out here. The front room has fielded panelling with bell-pushes all round, mostly original fixed seating and original window glass. More panelling in the rear room but only on one wall and the fireplace has gone. Through the double doors at the end of the L-shaped corridor is another inner lobby. Going back to the public bar, this has mostly intact fittings - the bar counter, island gantry-style bar back, fixed seating and glazed stone and wood fireplace. The Duke William Suite on the first floor is also worth a look.

Stoke-on-Trent, Burslem
21 Market Place, ST6 3AA
01782 819644
Grade II listed
LPA: Stoke-on-Trent

Leopard

An 18th-century building re-fronted around 1830 - but the early 20th-century fittings are the main point of interest. The passageway beyond the mosaic-floored entrance also has floor mosaic plus a mahogany partition with stained and leaded windows. In the front bar, the counter may well be original whilst the fixed seating in the rear lounge/dining room is also genuinely old. Downstairs, the leaded glass partition of the gents' is worth a look as are the ancient Adamant urinals. The Leopard has a tardis-like interior, including 53 bedrooms not used since 1951!

Staffordshire

Stoke-on-Trent, Dresden
34 Carlisle Street, ST3 4HA
01782 335488
Unlisted
LPA: Stoke-on-Trent

Princess Royal

A Victorian corner terrace pub with a multi-roomed interior. First up is the small, bare-boarded tap room with an old counter but modern top and bar back plus two windows etched 'Club Room'. Across the corridor, the snug is a good little room and has fixed seating and a cast-iron fireplace. Further on the left, the wide opening between the parlour and corridor looks suspiciously modern but it has been that way for very many years. Finally, the pool room at the back is a conversion from living quarters.

Stoke-on-Trent, Dresden
58 Peel Street, ST3 4PF
Unlisted
LPA: Stoke-on-Trent

Sir Robert Peel

This traditional back-street local is well worth seeking out for the spectacular bar back in the public bar. It dates probably to around 1870 and has four candy-twist columns and panels (formerly glass, now painted) advertising 'Fine Ales and Spirits'. The bar itself has much character, with its bare wood floor, Victorian bar counter with moulded top, some half-height panelling and what appears to be 1960s fixed seating. It has been knocked through to the games room behind. Observe also the rare 'Parkers Bitter Beer' window screens. The lounge on the right is greatly altered.

Stoke-on-Trent, Fenton
179 Whieldon Road, ST4 4JG
01782 255604
Unlisted
LPA: Stoke-on-Trent

Opens 3pm Monday-Thursday

Regent

This detached but now rather run-down 1930s Art Deco building has, to the right of the entrance lobby, a room retaining many original features. On show are a splendid, multi-coloured tiled floor, a sturdy bar counter unusually decorated with four rows of horizontal fielded panelling in broken strips and a mostly intact bar back. There is also fixed bench seating (newly upholstered) along the window wall and part of another. The front windows are curved in the Deco style and the original doors both to the lobby and toilets survive. The much-altered lounge bar to the left was once three rooms.

Right: the public bar at the Regent, a good survival from the 1930s, including the vibrant floor-tiling

Stoke-on-Trent, Hanley
65 Lichfield Street, ST1 3EA
01782 269445
Unlisted
LPA: Stoke-on-Trent

Opens 4pm Monday-Wednesday

Coachmakers Arms ★

A rare surviving example of an early Victorian mid-terrace pub which retains its layout of a central drinking passage with two rooms on either side. The passage has a tiled dado by Mintons, a red and black tiled floor and a hatch to the side of the servery. Old benches remain in the tiny snug bar (front left) but the original bar counter is somewhat marred by the over-large modern top. The lounge (front-right) has fixed bench seating and a period fireplace. At the rear right,

the small 'Piano Room' is quite plain except for an attractive, possibly Edwardian fire surround with pretty Art Nouveau touches; the red and black flooring is the same as in the corridor. Rear left is the most altered room, having been extended back into former private quarters. A threat of demolition because of redevelopment in the area hangs over the pub.

The lounge

Stoke-on-Trent, Hanley
65 Old Town Road, ST1 2JS
01782 212405
Grade II listed
LPA: Stoke-on-Trent

Golden Cup

A lovely little pub, built in 1912 and carefully restored in 2004. You are greeted by a superb green-tiled frontage celebrating Bass, then you find more tiles in both the entrance lobbies. The bar counter with fluted pilasters is superior Edwardian work, as is the delicate mirrored bar back whose superstructure is supported on elaborately turned posts surmounted by miniature acroteria. The snug, rear left, is a conversion from residential accommodation. Through an arch,

the rear right-hand room has old fixed upholstered seating with bell-pushes. Some of the original glass has been re-located.

The public bar is little altered since 1912

Stoke-on-Trent, Hanley

40 Piccadilly, ST1 1EG
01782 281809
Unlisted
LPA: Stoke-on-Trent

Unicorn

Many pubs were refitted in the 1960s but nearly all have had subsequent makeovers as tastes changed. This one-room town-centre local is an exception. The mock-Tudor fake beams and half-timbering on the walls are redolent of the time, as are the copper-topped bar counter, red upholstered fixed seating and copper-top tables. Before the 1960s there would have been two rooms here, hence the now out-of-use centrally-placed front door. The pub operates as the bar for the Regent theatre opposite - look for the order forms for interval drinks!

Stoke-on-Trent, Hartshill

296 Hartshill Road, ST4 7NH
01782 415731
Unlisted
LPA: Stoke-on-Trent

Jolly Potters

Built in 1827, this has the once common Potteries layout of four small rooms and a central passageway. The miniscule 'Victoria Ground Bar' (named after Stoke City's old ground) is the star attraction with its black and white tiled floor, old bar counter and bar-back shelves, half-height panelling and benches of uncertain vintage (though possibly early post-war). The colourful quarry-tiled passage has a hatch to the bar (but modern counter). The front-right snug has lost its door and fireplace and also its wall to the passageway - this was later reinstated, albeit with the upper part replaced by windows. The corner cupboard is the only old item. Rear right is the 'Teachers Lounge' with Victorian bench seating but no fireplace whilst the lounge rear left has some old panelling and less old seating.

Stoke-on-Trent, Northwood

19 Vincent Street, ST1 6PW
01782 268520
Unlisted
LPA: Stoke-on-Trent

Cross Guns

Until the early 1960s there were four small rooms here; since the conversion to two narrow bars then, little has changed. On the right, the public bar, with lino floor, has a plain counter and ply panels with shelves for a bar back. 1960s gas fires replaced the fireplaces. The carpeted lounge has a leatherette-fronted counter with Formica top and 1960s fixed seating but a modern fireplace. It's hard to argue there is much of architectural quality but plain, small drinkers' pubs like this are increasingly difficult to find.

Stoke-on-Trent, Penkhull

5-6 Manor Court Street,
ST4 5DW
01784 845978
Grade II listed
LPA: Stoke-on-Trent

Greyhound

In 1936 Parkers brewery of Burslem reconstructed this late 16th-century timber-framed building (formerly a court house) and its three-roomed interior hasn't changed much since. The lounge bar on the right has a fireplace from the original building plus a Tudor-arch fireplace from the 1936 work - the counter also seems to be from that time though the bar back is later. A doorway on the right brings you to a superb snug with walls completely covered with panelling from the first building. A tiled floor is beneath the carpet and the fireplace and fixed seating (with barley-twist arms and legs) are from the 1936 scheme. At the back, a small area with period fireplace has a door to a passage leading to the public bar. This has a dado of 1936 fielded panelling which extends to the counter front and the baffle by the front entrance and ceiling roses are also worthy of note (which is not the case with the fireplace and bar back).

Stoke-on-Trent, Pittshill (Tunstall)

13 Naylor Street, ST6 6LS
01782 834102
Grade II listed
LPA: Stoke-on-Trent
Open from 7.30pm and Sunday lunchtimes

Vine

An archetypal small, unspoilt back-street Victorian local with three little rooms. In northern towns and cities, hundreds if not thousands of such working-class pubs once existed but only a handful are still with us. A passageway runs from the front door with, on its left, a partly-glazed partition and two small rooms - a lounge at the front and a games room at the back, both with original fixed seating and 1950s tiled fireplaces. Opposite the games room is a hatch with a sliding window. The public bar on the right has an etched window inscribed 'Vaults' and original bar-back shelves, counter and fixed seating. The bar top and tiled fireplace are, however, later arrivals.

The Vine is a rare survival of an intact Victorian working man's pub. This is the public bar

The featured pubs in Birmingham city centre and surrounding suburbs

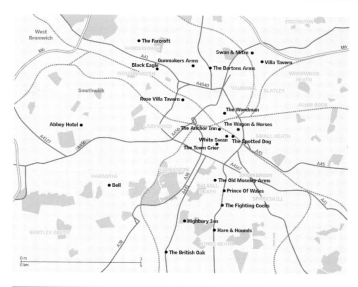

Birmingham, Aston

144 High Street,
Newtown, B6 4UP
0121 333 5988
Grade II* listed
LPA: Birmingham

Originally the smoke room, this part of the Bartons Arms has an extensive display of Minton Hollins tiling

Bartons Arms ★

This is one of the country's most impressive *fin-de-siècle* pubs. It dates from 1900-1 and was designed by James & Lister Lea for the brewers Mitchells & Butlers whose monogram appears in the glasswork. Built of stone and red brick in a wedge-shaped loosely Jacobean style, it's adorned with shaped gables and a tall clock tower. Alterations in 1980 opened up the interior somewhat but these spaces are still spectacular, due especially to the grand display of Minton Hollins tiling. At the sharp end of the building, two tiled vestibules access the public bar, originally divided into three by partitions. The more up-market areas were entered by another tiled vestibule facing the main road. Right of this was a saloon where the snob screens (to give higher class clients a sense of privacy) survive.

More snob screens occur in the great staircase-hall (pictured on the front cover) with its large tiled hunting scene. Left of the vestibule is a big smoke room with a projection to one side, now used for dining. On the stairwell is a fabulous stained glass window, dated 1901. Upstairs, the club and billiard rooms are still used for functions and meetings. The pub was closed for several years but was reopened in 2003.

83

Birmingham, Aston

305 Lichfield Road, B6 7ST

0121 326 0771

Grade II listed

LPA: Birmingham

Swan & Mitre

The fine brick and terracotta exterior here reveals the hands of those prolific local architects, James & Lister Lea, who rebuilt the pub for Holt's Brewery in 1898. The interior was well refurbished after vandalism in 1984 and the fittings in the main front bar are largely restored originals though the carved bar back with etched glass is probably a replica. The impressive bar counter has been truncated on the left though the decorated plaster ceiling and benches with mirrored glass above are

A fully tiled passage leads to the back of the Swan & Mitre

authentic. The lobby at the side and the rear tiled hall are unaltered but in the small rear smoke room, now used for pool, most of the old furniture has gone. Some excellent etched and stained glass windows do, though, survive both here and in the rear hall. There is also extensive floor-to-ceiling tiling in the rear passages and stairs.

Birmingham, Balsall Heath

53 Tindall Street, B12 9QU

0121 440 1954

Unlisted

LPA: Birmingham

Old Moseley Arms

Most of what you see in this three-roomed 19th-century inn dates from a comprehensive refit in the 1930s, though a later refurbishment in 1988 accounts for the bar back, and probably the counter, in the front-right room. Like the room behind it, this has fielded panelling to two-thirds height, a 1930s brick fireplace and old fixed seating (above which are bell-pushes in the room behind). The

left-hand bar has panelling, fireplace and seating from the same era. The sloping bar counter is also from that time as is the Art Deco part-mirrored bar-back fitting.

The left-hand bar dates from a refit in the 1930s

Birmingham, Bearwood

Abbey Road, B67 5RA
0121 429 6067
Grade II listed
LPA: Sandwell

Abbey Hotel

This huge roadhouse was built in 1931 to a neo-Georgian design by Wood & Kendrick for Mitchells & Butlers. Predictably, much opening out and modernisation has subsequently taken place but sufficient remains to give a good idea of its former splendour. The public bar is dominated by a long bar counter and a mirrored bar back with paired pilasters and a pedimented central bay. The wall formerly separating it from the smoke room has been removed. A separate side entrance leads into a hall with a smoke room off to the right. Ahead is a cavernous dining room/lounge where the counter and bar back at the far end have replaced a hatch to a servery behind. A loggia in the garden is currently boarded up and out of use.

The public bar

Birmingham, Bordesley Green

28 Adderley Street, B9 4ED
0121 772 1403
Unlisted
LPA: Birmingham

Waggon & Horses

The last major revamp here was in 1978 with the removal of the off-sales, the only real change to the layout. In the public bar, the 1930s bar back is decorated with green and cream tiles and there are some good patterned windows. A Victorian counter survives in both this bar and the rear smoke room. Access to the smoke room, formerly via a passage on the right, is now through an archway from the bar and the room still has its old fixed seating.

Birmingham, Digbeth

308 Bradford Street, B5 6ET
0121 622 4516
Grade II listed
LPA: Birmingham

Anchor ★

A red-brick and terracotta pub built in 1902 for Ansells' brewery to the designs of renowned local pub architects, James & Lister Lea. Inside, a timber and glass screen divides the main public bar; a plan on display in the smoke room shows that this was one of several which formerly split up the interior into small compartments, including an off-sales accessed from Rea Street. The original counter and bar back make up an L-shaped servery, with heating pipes running along the foot of the counter. The smoke room (now called 'lounge') behind has a hatch, modern counter, etched panels in the doors and fixed seating with baffles and bell-pushes. Between this room and the Rea Street entrance is a charming small drinking area. Typical of many of the city's pubs from this era is the Art Nouveau-style detail in the upper windows and geometric patterned glass in the lower ones.

Partitions often divided up Victorian public bars in Birmingham. This is a rare survivor

85

Fewer but Better

The sheer number of pubs in our towns and cities was a matter of concern to many, especially those of Temperance persuasion. It was perceived as a major cause of drunkenness, especially in the large number of 'low, small, not secret houses' of inner urban areas. In 1896 Birmingham had no less than 1,703 beerhouses and full-licensed public houses. Back in 1877 the Council persuaded itself to take over the drink trade, just as it had other utilities. Mayor Joseph Chamberlain, who had successfully municipalized gas and water supply, proclaimed 'I want to treat the drink question as we have treated the gas question.' In fact nothing came of this and it fell to Joseph's brother Arthur, as Chairman of the licensing magistrates from 1894, to start the process of license reduction through the innovative Birmingham Surrender Scheme.

This was a voluntary compensation scheme created in 1897 by a group of brewers in Birmingham and members of the Birmingham Licensing Committee who formed the Birmingham Property Company. This purchased old run-down houses in the centre of the city with multiple licenses being surrendered to build, as the slogan associated with the scheme put it, 'fewer but better' pubs further out. The scheme established a fund which compensated those giving up licenses and it was copied in other towns such as Sheffield and Blackburn. In Birmingham about forty licenses a year were given up between 1898 and 1903.

Then the Licensing Act of 1904 provided a national framework for license reduction. Closures, except those made because of bad conduct or structural unsoundness, were to be compensated from a fund levied on all licensed properties. In all some 600 on-licences nationally a year were removed between 1905 and 1935.

Geoff Brandwood

The Red Lion, Vicarage Road, King's Heath, of 1903-4 is one of the great classics among 'improved' public houses. It was built by an estate company to serve middle-class housing. This kind of establishment aimed to give pubs greater respectability. Tragically the original interior no longer exists.

Rooms in the historic pub

Until the late 20th century pubs almost invariably consisted of two or more public rooms.

Romping Cat, Bloxwich

They varied in the quality of surroundings on offer and with this went a differential in pricing. You paid less for your beer in the public bar which was the most simply appointed and often very much a male preserve. This was the domain of the working man. Here there would be a bar counter, no carpet on the floor, lots of smoke in the air, and the standard drink would be mild (which has now all but disappeared from our pubs). The public bar was

White Swan, Birmingham

sometimes termed the vaults, especially in the north (however, the Bell, Bloxwich, p.96, has a vaults). Better-appointed rooms went under a variety of names. Private bars (more common in London than the Midlands) did not involve a requirement of

membership (after all they were in public houses) but were smaller than public bars and the name suggests occupancy by regulars known to one another. The snug was similar – a smallish, cosy space. The lounge and saloon tended to be larger and one might expect carpets, panelling and service at your table (see p.28). Much the same

Victoria, Beeston

might be expected in the smoke/smoking room. These latter names are a little mysterious since there was no restriction on

smoking throughout a pub. Maybe the idea was to suggest somewhere where people could take their ease in the way they would have done in a

White Horse,
Leamington Spa

smoking room of a gentleman's residence?

Then there were club rooms, function rooms, music rooms, billiard rooms and off-sales compartments, for all of which the purpose is self-evident. Commercial and news rooms featured more in the north than the Midlands and were places where one

might do business or relax for a quiet read. One puzzling name, however, is the tap room. One might be forgiven for thinking that this was where drinks were dispensed but examination of

Villa Tavern, Birmingham

old plans of pubs, and the evidence from ones where tap rooms exist, shows this was not the case in the vast majority of instances because the room was separated from, and often at a fair distance from, the servery (an exception was at the now-closed Shakespeare, Dudley, West Midlands, where

what we would normally call the public bar was known as the tap room). One long-serving licensee has suggested that in tap rooms regulars would tap a coin or their glass to attract attention to summon service. Well, maybe!

Geoff Brandwood

Birmingham, Digbeth
104 Warwick Street, B12 0NH
0121 772 3822
Unlisted
LPA: Birmingham

Opens 5pm Monday-Thursday,
3pm Friday

Spotted Dog

A small 1930s corner pub which retains three rooms though the two at the front are now connected by a wide opening rather than a door. The right-hand of these bars is fairly plain with simple multi-shelved bar back, original counter, bench seating and Art Deco fireplace. The next bar has a minimalist bar back and original counter, a dado and two benches - the dog window is a recent replacement for a corner door. The third room, at a right angle, has a similar bar back and counter, half-height-panelling and bench seating. Modest but charming.

Birmingham, Digbeth
34 Macdonald Street, B5 6TG
0121 622 4423
Unlisted
LPA: Birmingham

Town Crier

The austere exterior, with modern UPVC windows, of this early 1960s pub promises little but inside surprisingly little has changed. From the entrance corridor, the public bar is on the right and has original furniture and benches, bar shelving and counter, though there is some more recent timberwork attached to the counter and side wall. At the back is a little-used lounge/function room with fake timbered walls.

Birmingham, Digbeth
276 Bradford Street, B12 0QY
0121 622 2586
Grade II listed
LPA: Birmingham

The public bar, White Swan

White Swan ★

The prolific local pub architects James & Lister Lea designed this ambitious red-brick and terracotta corner pub of 1899-1900 for Ansells' brewery. The tiled corridor on the left-hand side is a joy to behold and widens into a stand-up drinking area with a serving hatch (see p.42). The L-shaped public bar sits in the angle of the roads and has its original counter and bar back, the latter with a distinctive balustrade on top. Tiling covers the walls, including a pretty, swirling cornice similar to that in the corridor, whilst the ceiling is covered in copper tiles, albeit now painted over. The main internal changes are the loss of two low partitions in the public bar and insertion of a modern counter in the smoke room. The off-sales, closed in 2005, still exists but is used for storage.

Birmingham, Digbeth

New Canal Street, B5 5LG

0121 643 4960

Grade II listed

LPA: Birmingham

Woodman ★

Reopened in 2013 after restoration by sympathetic new owners. Built in 1896-7 for Ansells' Brewery, this is one of the finest of the many Birmingham tiled and terracotta pubs designed by James & Lister Lea. It stood, for many years, unloved in an urban wasteland but recent developments around it helped to secure its future. The main bar, now one room, but once two split by a partition, is dominated by the splendid bar counter and even grander bar back. The room has much excellent Minton tiling. To the right is a small drinking corridor, also sumptuously tiled. An angled door leads to the true marvel which is the smoke room, with more glorious wall-tiling, a lovely marble fireplace, an old mirror set into the tiles, bench seating all round and a large hatch to the bar with glazed panel above. Returning to the main bar, and ahead of the corner entrance, a snug occupies what had been a plain back room, which was brought into pub use at a later date.

The smoke room at the rear of the Woodman is a remarkable room, retaining its fittings and full-height tiling from 1896-7

Birmingham, Erdington

71-73 Summer Road, B23 6UT

0121 384 2918

Unlisted

LPA: Birmingham

New Inns

Behind the excellent brown faience frontage of this Edwardian pub lies, firstly, a good plain bar with vestibule entrance and original counter and carved bar back. To the left, a passage has a timber and etched glass partition to the bar. The bar fittings in the rear lounge are modern but the cornices and the bench seating with bell-pushes above are original. Further back is a small area with more old bench seating and a tiled fireplace.

Birmingham, Erdington
105 Station Road, B23 6UG
0121 373 0373
Unlisted
LPA: Birmingham

The ceramic bar counter in the public bar

Red Lion

This corner pub of 1899, with a prominent square clock tower, was designed by Wood & Kendrick for Mitchells & Butlers. In the public bar, a superb servery sweeps round through 90 degrees, fronted by a stunning ceramic bar counter by Craven Dunnill of Jackfield, Shropshire. The lavish bar-back features a corner clock, glittering ornamented glasswork and a large, unusual mirror. The bar floor is modern. A flimsy stud partition forms the right-hand wall and it's said that until quite recently an off-sales lay beyond and the counter was cut back - but how this fits together is hard to comprehend. The large saloon/smoke room beyond looks little altered but this seems unlikely (there is certainly a disused external doorway on the right but it is far removed from the supposed off-sales). Anyway, away from these mysteries, this room has a good bar back (but modern counter) and generous semi-circular seating units.

Birmingham, Handsworth
Rookery Road, B21 9QY
0121 554 0957
Unlisted
LPA: Birmingham

Farcroft

This mighty essay in 'Brewers' Tudor' is one of Birmingham's largest inter-war pubs, but it's an early example, built around 1921 by Holt's Brewery. The vast public bar, with high decorated ceilings, is split in two by an original timber partition. It has two doorways, both with plain timber lobbies, though the rear one is out of use. The counter of the large L-shaped servery is original, as is the carved bar back with mirrors and a corner clock (but a few new shelves added). At the back is a now modernised small square lounge along with function rooms.

Birmingham, Harborne
11 Old Church Road, B17 0BB
0121 428 4609
Grade II listed
LPA: Birmingham

Bell

The age of this building is difficult to judge as it has clearly evolved over many years but it has been a pub since around 1862, when this would still have been a rural location. The spine is a central corridor with red-tiled floor and timber dado plus, on the left, a remarkably small counter to the servery which has been formed at the bottom of the stairs. Rear left is a snug with fixed seating, more red-tiled flooring, glazed hatch to servery and a vast fireplace. The big room on the right probably took its present form in the inter-war period - the fixed seating and abundance of half-timbering is certainly typical of that era. At the back is a well-tended bowling green with an unusual L-shape.

Birmingham, Hockley
16 Factory Road, B18 5JU
0121 523 4008
Unlisted
LPA: Birmingham

Black Eagle

Built in 1895, this pub has five small rooms, four of them clustered round a central servery. The bar front left has its original counter (incorporating a row of Minton tiles) and bar back and this also serves the tap room on the right. The lounge at the front-right has absorbed the former off-sales; it has its original counter but some tiles were damaged and the rest re-used on the rear smoke room counter. The former entrance to this room is blocked up and the fixed seating in front of it is modern, the rest being original. In the rear smoke room the counter has been enlarged to the right. The bar-back fitting actually consists of what were the exterior windows, removed to create the doorway to the rear dining room (which has no old fittings). On the right are a 1920s tiles and wood surround fireplace and inter-war fixed seating.

Birmingham, Hockley
172 Warstone Lane, B18 6JW
0121 236 7910
Grade II listed
LPA: Birmingham

This pub features all-over tiling from 1920

Rose Villa Tavern ★

This 1919-20 pub was designed by Mitchells & Butlers' regular architects, Wood & Kendrick, and is in a style interestingly poised between florid late-Victorian taste and the simpler architecture of the post-war years. The significant internal changes make it now possible to circumnavigate the central servery. The extensive tilework by Carters of Poole is the star attraction though. It is at its most dramatic in the small room behind the servery with its floor-to-ceiling tiling and embellishments round the inglenook fireplace; the tile painting over the fireplace and the stained glass in the skylight are also

endearing. Plenty of tiling, also, in the main front bar, including panels depicting scantily-clad damsels (two more of which are in the former off-sales passage but the use of the area for storage makes them difficult to view). The exterior window glass, too, is a highlight with its colourful representations of galleons (a long way from the sea here). The pub reopened in 2011 after refurbishment which added various contemporary design features for better or worse.

Birmingham, King's Heath
106 High Street, B14 7JZ
0121 444 2081
Grade II listed
LPA: Birmingham

Hare & Hounds

The special feature here is the spectacular display of floor-to-ceiling Art Nouveau-style tiling by Maw & Co., especially in the hallway and stairs accessed from the York Road entrance. The dado tiling demonstrates the company's tube-lining technique in which areas of colour are separated by thin ribbons of clay. Above the dado, with its floral motifs, are creamy green tiles broken by strips of flower forms. The public bar is now one L-shaped room but until 1983 there was a series of separate bars on the High Street side. The clock, complete with Holt Brewery squirrel, is a notable feature. The mahogany bar counter and bar back have both been tinkered with but much survives. The rear lounge used to be two little smoke rooms - again the bar back is mostly original as is the splendid fireplace. The upstairs rooms also have some genuine old elements.

Although the rest of the building is much altered, the hallway at the Hare & Hounds, with its mosaic floor, wall-tiles and woodwork, is a superb example of Edwardian pub-fitting. The date is 1906-7.

Birmingham, Lozells
123 Gerrard Street, B19 1DP
0121 507 1774
Grade II listed
LPA: Birmingham

Gunmakers Arms

A pretty brick and terracotta pub of 1902-3 designed by M.J.Butcher for Ansells' Brewery. This pub has extensive wall-tiling and it also had a splendid ceramic bar counter. However, most of the counter was stolen in 1996 whilst the pub was closed and only a small section in the rear lounge is now left. In the L-shaped front bar, a decorative, multi-coloured tiled dado adorns the lower walls with beige tiles above rising to the ceiling. Similar tiles enrich the lobby and passage. At the back, the lounge has unfortunate 1960s 'beamed' walls but the counter makes up for this.

Right: The Craven Dunnill counter in the rear lounge (see Index, Ceramic counters for other examples)

Birmingham, Moseley
1 St Mary's Row,
Alcester Road, B13 8JG
0121 449 0811
Grade II listed
LPA: Birmingham

Fighting Cocks

Built in 1898-9 by architects Newton & Cheatle for Holt's Brewery, the Fighting Cocks has endured various corporate refurbishments, including Firkin branding in the 1990s and Goose branding later - but it's still a fabulous building, inside and out. The superb brick and stone exterior is in a mixed Tudor/Arts & Crafts style with a clock tower, big stained and leaded glass windows and a barometer and windspeed indicator by the corner entrance. Inside, the three rooms surround a central servery which has a fine heavy mahogany gantry, etched mirrors and good plain counter. Along the front are original timber entrance lobbies with etched glass. The L-shaped corner bar has green Craven Dunnill wall tiles and a decorative ceiling. The modernised lounge retains two picture-tile panels (see p.2), one showing a pub called the Fighting Cocks, no doubt the current building's predecessor, and the other a church in a rural setting - is there more beneath the wallpaper?

Birmingham, Moseley
118 Alcester Road, B13 8EE
0121 449 4198
Unlisted
LPA: Birmingham

Prince of Wales

An excellent community boozer with several rooms. The plain bar across the front has an especially good bar back with etched and gilded mirrors plus an old panelled counter (somewhat shortened) and benches. The two doors from the lobby indicate that there were once separate rooms here. Behind the servery, with service through a hatch-counter, is a long corridor with brick-tiled floor and original window panels at the end. Two small lounges lie off this passage, both plushly and traditionally decorated and with good ceilings and, in one case, panelling and bell-pushes above the seats plus an ornate fireplace.

Birmingham, Nechells
307 Nechells Park Road,
B7 5PD
0121 326 7466
Grade II listed
LPA: Birmingham

Villa Tavern ★

A red-brick and terracotta corner pub built for Ansells in 1924-5 to designs by Matthew J. Butcher. The public bar occupies the angle of the site and retains its counter and bar back, the latter with round arches and mirror glass. Typical 1920s dado tiling decorates the lobby area between bar and club room. Behind the servery, the small smoke room is complete with fixed seating, bell-pushes and old fireplace (but new bar counter). Some original seating clings on in the club room. The sign outside saying 'Built 1897' is simply wrong!

Birmingham, Northfield
Bristol Road South, B31 2QT
0121 477 1800
Grade II listed
LPA: Birmingham

The downstairs hall

Black Horse ★

Indisputably one of the most magnificent pubs created between the wars, this enormous 'Brewers' Tudor' roadhouse was rebuilt in 1929 for local brewers Davenports by Francis Goldborough of architects Bateman & Bateman. The extravagantly half-timbered exterior sports gables, carved woodwork, leaded glass and barley-sugar chimneys. Inside, the ground floor has experienced much change, especially at the front, including from its latest incarnation as a J.D.Wetherspoon outlet. The most notable ground-floor spaces are the former gents' smoke room (rear right) and the dining and assembly room (rear left); the former is a romantic evocation of a baronial hall with a sturdy tie-beam roof (the servery is modern), while the latter has a series of low ceilings, punctuated by tall, two-light windows. Among the details to enjoy on the ground floor are three grand and varied fireplaces. Upstairs is less changed and definitely worth seeing. A barrel-vaulted lobby area leads to a huge function room (with three-sided ceiling) and, beyond this, a conference room with a fine circular plaster ceiling. Don't miss the spacious bowling green at the back.

Birmingham, Stirchley
1364 Pershore Road, B30 2XS
0121 458 1758
Grade II listed
LPA: Birmingham

British Oak ★

An excellent, largely intact inter-war pub of 1923-4, designed by prolific local pub architects, James & Lister Lea. The brick-built, asymmetrical frontage is in 17th-century domestic style with, behind,

The rear smoke room

no less than five substantially intact public rooms. Central double doors lead into a lobby, with tiled dado, behind which the large public bar has a terrazzo floor, original fixed seating and oak bar counter; the original bar back is also still there but has been painted yellow. Front left, the formerly gents-only narrow lounge contains its original fireplace and panelling, fixed seating with bell-pushes and a couple of baffles. To the rear is the assembly room with parquet floor, marble fireplace and small hatch to the servery. In the smoke room, also at the back, you'll find wall-panelling to two-thirds height and a three-sided servery which may be original. Returning to the front of the building,

The public bar is very much as built in 1923-4. The floor is of patterned terrazzo

the right-hand room also retains its old fireplace and seating. Fine tiling in the toilets. The bowling green is still used.

Birmingham, Stirchley
Dads Lane, B13 8PQ
0121 472 8630
Unlisted
LPA: Birmingham

Highbury

A typical large Birmingham suburban pub, built in the 1920s for Mitchells & Butlers. The public bar at the front corner of the pub still has its original counter, an elegant bar back (with 'M&B' carved in the pediment), wall-panelling to two-thirds height, and a decorated fireplace. The door to the rear lounge has given way to a wider opening and this room is now used for pool. The wall-panelling here is a little more elaborate and the beams are decorated. The small curved counter is probably from the 1950s or 1960s. A separate side entrance leads to a mostly modernised lounge (formerly gents only in the days when it was still legal to exclude women from parts of a pub) and a plain function room with panelled walls and a segmental-shaped ceiling. A former off-license can also be discerned between the two entrances.

Bloxwich

1 Bell Lane, WS3 2JN

01922 405990

Unlisted

LPA: Walsall

Bell

This is an early 20th-century corner-site pub with rooms leading off a central corridor. The door to the public bar bears the name 'Vaults', an alternative term quite commonly used in the past. It still has its original counter, bar back and fixed seating though the tiled floor is new. The smoke room (with an etched door window) has old fixed seating as has the games room. In the passage, a hatch has a sliding window. The inner half-doors have etched panels.

Bloxwich

97 Elmore Green Road, WS3 2HN

01922 475041

Grade II listed

LPA: Walsall

The plan of the public bar and its bar counter follow the sweep of the external wall

Romping Cat ★

A corner local of 1900, still retaining its three-room layout and 'outdoor department' (whose sliding sash windows still function). In the right-hand bar are an unaltered bar counter, bar back and fixed seating plus etched and frosted windows. The small smoke room on the left has a hatch to the servery and original bench seating but a modern fireplace within the old wooden surround. Running round the back of the servery, a passage with colourful mosaic flooring leads to a further bar with an etched window (inscribed 'Coffee Room'), intact old fireplace and original, if shortened, seating. The pub was once the Sandbank Tavern but its nickname, derived from the heraldic lion on the sign, became official in 1957.

Bloxwich

13 Wolverhampton Road,
WS3 2EZ
01922 407745
Grade II listed
LPA: Walsall

Opens 7pm Monday-Thursday

Turf Tavern ★

Described, with much justification, as 'the last truly unspoilt terraced pub left in the country', the Turf has been in the same family since 1871. Beyond the central entrance, the quarry-tiled passage has, on the right-hand side, two hatches to the servery. The public bar is also quarry-tiled and features a simple Victorian bar back (with drawers) and counter (but with 1960s Formica top) plus handpumps dating from 1927. The bare fixed seating is supplemented with a couple of simple, moveable low benches.

The front left-hand room has window glass inscribed 'Smoke Room', 'Wines' and 'Spirits'; the fixed seating is unusual with its padded benches divided into individual seats by arm rests. The rear-left room has leather-covered bench seating with baffles. The outside gents' are worth a visit and other outbuildings include the malt room of the former home brewery and three pigsties.

The unspoilt public bar at the Turf Tavern

Brierley Hill

10 Delph Road, DY5 2TN
01384 78293
Unlisted
LPA: Dudley

Vine ('Bull & Bladder')

A renowned four-roomer, attached to Batham's Brewery, and rebuilt in 1912 because of subsidence. The small front bar on the right is splendidly unaltered, retaining the Edwardian counter, bar back, fixed seating and terrazzo floor. Front left, the two-part room has been extended and modernised but still has old bench seating and an inter-war fireplace - the stained and leaded windows are also notable. A terrazzo passage from the front door leads to a small room, rear left, with old tiled fireplace and later bench seating. The rear-right room is an inter-war convert from domestic use and retains fittings from that time.

The public bar is scarcely changed since the rebuilding of 1912

97

Coventry

214 Binley Road, Copsewood,
CV3 1HG

024 7644 3196

Unlisted

LPA: Coventry

Biggin Hall Hotel

A suburban pub/hotel built in 1923 in 'Brewers' Tudor' style. The front bar has been knocked about a bit, including shortening of the bar counter and installation of a new bar back - it has also been extended to incorporate the former off-sales area . The corridor area is served by a small curved, glazed counter. The rear right-hand room has a fine array of panelling but was opened out to the corridor in

2005. The large back room is opulently panelled and dominated by a magnificent inglenook fireplace. The counter is original (but the bar back is new) as are the leaded windows, bench seating and some of the tables and chairs - the coffin-shaped table in the middle of the room is worthy of note. Some inter-war fittings can also be found in the upstairs function room, an amalgamation of formerly separate rooms.

Original fittings and furnishings from
1923 in the main rear room

Coventry

22 Spon Street, CV1 3BA

024 7625 1717

Grade II listed

LPA: Coventry

Old Windmill

A 16th-century building, entered down a long, flagged, panelled corridor. A small room on the left has inter-war panelling and fireplace plus a hatch to the bar. To the right is a delightful suite of three small rooms. First is a snug with recent panelling and a curious copper-topped counter. The gem of a second room is entered through a narrow door and has ancient panelling, old leaded windows, a splendid black-brick open fire and a patterned tiled floor. The third room has been opened out on both sides though the skeleton of one

wall survives. It has a very large and fine fireplace. The area further back is a former yard now covered with a glass roof. A former outbuilding, containing the remains of an old brewery, has been incorporated into the pub.

The second room on the right
is one of several historic
spaces at the Old Windmill

Netherton

89 Halesowen Road, DY2 9PY

01384 253075

Grade II listed

LPA: Dudley

Old Swan ('Ma Pardoe's') ★

One of only four brew-pubs still operating when CAMRA was formed in 1971, this Black Country institution takes its nickname from Mrs Doris Pardoe, licensee until 1984. Brewing stopped in 1988 but restarted in 2001. The wonderfully evocative front bar seems unchanged since Victorian times (aside from the vibrant red paint). The enamel-panel ceiling is an extraordinary rarity and its eponymous swan is a striking feature, as are the old stove (still used) with its flue running across the room, and the old weighing machine. Historic fittings are also found in the rear smoke room, originally entered from a corridor door on the right. The drinking area right of the smoke room was converted out of a former office in the 1980s. Between the two old bars is a wee off-sales-cum-snug with a single bench for customers wanting a swift one after making their take-out purchase. The 1980s changes also saw expansion into the shop next door but without compromising the historic core.

The public bar may date back as far as the 1860s. In addition to its Victorian servery, it is notable for the remarkable enamelled ceiling which depicts the eponymous swan

Oldbury

17a Church Street, B69 3AD

0121 552 5467

Grade II listed

LPA: Sandwell

Waggon & Horses

A corner pub built about 1900 by Holt's Brewery in the brick and terracotta style so typical of the area. When it comes to internal tiling, it's in the top league anywhere. On the corner, as usual, is the public bar with mainly cream tiles but also colourful bands lining the walls and a richly-treated bar back no doubt dating from the building of the pub. The ceiling is remarkable for being clad with sheet copper tiles, unfortunately painted over more than once. The side entrance leads to a fabulous tiled corridor, with a hatch to the servery, which makes an L-shape round a smoke room with original fixed seating, plentiful bell-pushes and a 1930s tiled and wood surround fireplace. Closed as of writing this guide, but expected to reopen by the time it is published.

Tiling and a copper ceiling grace the public bar

Rushall

Park Road, Daw End, WS4 1LG

01922 642333

Grade II listed

LPA: Walsall

Manor Arms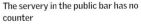

Here is one of the very few pubs in the UK with no bar counter. A three-room canal-side establishment, it opened as a beerhouse in 1895 within an older building. Many regulars favour the central corridor for drinking and on its left is the public bar, with handpumps and taps set against the back wall beneath rows of shelving for glasses and bottles. Customers and serving staff are not therefore segregated as is the case with a conventional bar counter. This warm and welcoming room has simple dado panelling, a boarded ceiling, fixed bench seating and a (possibly) inter-war fireplace. The front-right room has an old quarry-tiled floor, fixed seating and a modern brick fireplace in an old inglenook. The lounge at the back entered pub use only quite recently.

The servery in the public bar has no counter

Sedgley

129 Bilston Street, DY3 1JE

01902 883380

Grade II listed

LPA: Dudley

The smoke room with its remarkable glazed-in servery

Beacon Hotel

An unspoilt gem of a four-room pub with a still-functioning mid-Victorian tower brewery at the back. Little has changed since Sarah Hughes bought the business in 1921, other than extra rooms being created at the rear. Most remarkable is the small glazed-in cubicle for service sitting between the front snug and the larger rear smoke room. Both these rooms have small hatches for service as does the corridor and each hatch requires customers to bend down to communicate their needs to staff. In the large smoke room, the

boarding was covered up for many years, being revealed in a 1987 refurbishment - it may well be Victorian. The front tap room might once have been a kitchen (observe the range) and some fittings look Victorian. The brewery lay idle from the 1950s until 1987, since when it has produced award-winning ales whose names commemorate the redoubtable Sarah Hughes.

Stourbridge

Lower High Street, DY8 1TS

01384 395374

Unlisted

LPA: Dudley

Mitre

Occupying an awkward, wedge-shaped site, this imposing example of 'Brewers' Tudor' has especially good original leaded and painted windows all round - these have an important influence inside as well, being ornamented with heraldic designs and, of course, the eponymous mitre. The rest of the interior has suffered from low-grade alterations over the years but some old features are still in place. The triangular servery reflects the shape of the site but it's difficult to work out the former arrangements of the now-interlinked rooms surrounding it. Apart from the public bar, they were no doubt quite small. The aforementioned old features include the dumb waiter in the servery, carved bar counter with glazed screen behind, and panelling in a couple of rooms. The fireplaces - two stone, one timber-framed and one brick - make an interesting collection.

Seven Stars

Stourbridge
22 Brook Road, DY8 1NQ
01384 396643
Unlisted
LPA: Dudley

Built in 1907 for Mitchells & Butlers Brewery, the Seven Stars has an outstanding collection of M&B etched and painted windows. The entrance hall has lots of light blue and cream dado tiling, which extends up the stairs and into the public bar. That room has its original counter and a superb four-bay, mirrored bar back with a clock-adorned pediment. Below the pediment is a recently reopened hatch to the smoke room behind. This is modernised but bell-pushes remain above the benches as do fine etched windows. The restaurant left of the hallway has nothing of historic interest apart from a couple of windows.

Britannia ★

Upper Gornal
109 Kent Street, DY3 1UX
01902 883253
Unlisted
LPA: Dudley

The interest here focuses on the very special room rear-left, possibly fitted out in the 1920s. The 'wood' panelling is in fact imitation and there are fixed benches and some stained glass. The real highlights, though, are the shelving, drawers and bank of four handpumps set against the corridor wall - a hugely rare arrangement of a servery without a counter (and still used Saturday nights). The hatch with pewter ledge to the corridor would probably have been used as an off-sales and also by customers in the second room, now taken up by the ladies' toilet. The rest of the pub wasn't then in public use, the present servery area being a butcher's shop until Batham's bought and extended the pub in 1997. Also known as 'Sallies' after the landlady from 1942 to 1991.

This room at the Britannia was fitted up perhaps in the 1920s: service is from the handpumps on the left

Rose & Crown

Walsall, Birchills
55 Old Birchills, WS2 8QH
01922 720533
Grade II listed
LPA: Walsall

Constructed in 1901 for Highgate Brewery, this former small hotel was sympathetically refurbished in 1999. Passing through a full-height, etched screen, you enter a very fine drinking passage with a multi-coloured tiled dado round most of it and a hatch to the bar. On the left, the sizeable public bar has original counter, bar back and fixed seating plus a tiled

The servery, 1901

frieze round four-fifths of the room. More tiles adorn the counter front. To the right of the passage are two rooms between which doorways were cut some years back. The 1999 refit added a small piece of new fixed seating to the original benches in the front room to block off one doorway. The rear room has no old fittings.

Walsall

5 John Street, WS2 8AF

01922 612553

Unlisted

LPA: Walsall

Pretty Bricks

Known as the Pretty Bricks because of its very attractive glazed-brick frontage, this 1840-built pub was much altered in 1924 and most of the resulting features are still there. The entrance leads into a passage (with the front bar off to the right) which opens out into a rear lobby, then a rear lounge with a new fireplace. In the centre is an irregularly shaped servery (not quite its original layout), with good stained glass screens on the lounge side.

Wednesbury

56 Bridge Street, WS10 0AH

0121 5020826

Unlisted

LPA: Sandwell

Coachmakers

A small Victorian local whose fine faience frontage sports a lovely tiled panel advertising 'Woodhall's Old English Ales'. Inside, most of the original layout is intact but somewhat spoilt by tacky DIY alterations incorporating 'beams' and Artex. The small front bar has a good original counter, plain bar back and inter-war fireplace. Attractive tiled dado and panelling in the side passage while the small rear lounge , with a part-glazed partition wall to the passage, is served via a hatch and retains original bench seating.

Wednesbury

Wood Green Road, WS10 9AX

0121 505 7182

Unlisted

LPA: Sandwell

The Horse & Jockey is one of three pubs in this guide with ceramic bar counters (see Index, Ceramic counters)

Horse & Jockey ★

Built in 1898 to designs by Wood & Kendrick, this otherwise much-altered pub is notable for the spectacular servery in the public bar. It has a ceramic bar counter organised in a series of layers, as if on a cake, each with different colour and detail. Dividing the counter into a series of bays are brown pilasters, each topped by gargoyles with protruding tongues. Sadly, the counter, which previously continued to the wall, has been cut back on the left . Behind is an elaborately-treated back-fitting of five bays housing some fine mirror-work. This bar once had a central partition with a door in the middle. The large back room is mostly modern and is an enlargement of the former smoke room.

Wednesbury

19 Hall End, WS10 9ED

0121 556 0197

Grade II listed

LPA: Sandwell

Old Blue Ball

The layout of this small Victorian pub is relatively unaltered, the last changes probably dating from the 1970s. From the entrance corridor, with its tiled floor and hatch service, a plain front bar is on the right and has an old counter with mosaic glass front (perhaps applied in the 1970s) and plain old bar shelves with delicate spindle supports and mosaic glass. Across the corridor, the room now extending front to back was once two snugs and only the benches survive. Rear right, behind the servery, the small snug was converted from living quarters in the 1970s.

Wednesfield

35 Lichfield Road, WV11 1TN

01902 733529

Grade II listed

LPA: Wolverhampton

Vine ★

A rare and intact example of a simple inter-war, urban, working-class pub. It was designed in 1937 by architects Watkin & Maddox of Burslem for Truman, Hanbury & Buxton: it opened in 1938. The only changes have been the loss of the off-sales hatch opposite the front door and insertion of a tiny counter in the smoke room. The public bar has a colourful terrazzo floor plus the original bar counter, seating and fireplace. To the right is the smoke room with parquet floor, Tudor-style fireplace and fixed seating with bell-pushes. A second smoke room lies at the back across the terrazzo-floored hallway and has similar features. The toilets are also scarcely altered since construction. The anachronistic Victorian-style embossed paper applied to the dados is the only jarring note.

The public bar retains its original 1937 fittings and terrazzo floor

Willenhall

77 Gomer Street West,
WV13 2NR
01902 633378
Unlisted
LPA: Wolverhampton

Falcon

Since it was constructed in 1936, only the lounge has seen significant modernisation. The corridor leading all the way through from the front door has a splendid, boldly-patterned tiled floor and half-height terrazzo wall-tiling. The same flooring extends into the excellent public bar which has embossed wallpaper on the walls and ceiling, a heavily embossed frieze with vaguely organic patterns, a sturdy pine bar counter with matching bar back and plentiful original bench seating. In the same family ownership for over 30 years.

Like the Vine (opposite page), the public bar at the Falcon has kept its 1930s fittings and has a showy terrazzo floor

Wolverhampton, City Centre

90 Chapel Ash, WV3 0TY
01902 421880
Unlisted
LPA: Wolverhampton

Combermere Arms

Built in 1860 but the current layout mainly dates from alterations in 1925. To the left of the central corridor (which has hatch service) is the main bar, which suffers from crude post-war interventions. The best rooms are the two snugs on the other side of the corridor - one in lounge-style with simple fireplace and benches, the other plainer with red-tiled floor and brick fireplace. A substantial tree grows within the outside gents!

Wolverhampton, City Centre

48 Lichfield Street, WV1 1DG
07967 185830
Grade II listed
LPA: Wolverhampton

Posada

An elegant town-centre pub of 1886 though the notable faience frontage is from a 1900 remodelling by local architect Fred T. Beck. The public bar, entered through a vestibule added in 1983, is a very special room with its fabulous tiled walls and ornate bar-back fitting, the latter with mirrored panels and a row of snob screens, now very rare in British pubs. Above them are three glazed panels with green Art Nouveau motifs.

The elaborate bar back at the Posada

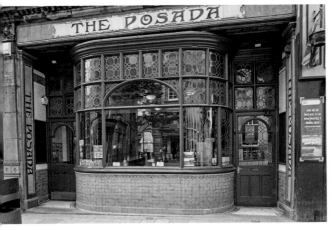

The ornate plasterwork ceiling is now painted brown. In 1983, an opening was created to the rear smoke room, previously accessed by a passageway running behind the bar back (still there but used for storage). This room retains a good proportion of its old fixed seating with bell-pushes above; the 1983 alterations created an alcove on the right in what had been the rear passageway and an access was cut through to a new, small room at the back. Despite these changes, there is much to cherish here.

Posada, Wolverhampton

Wolverhampton, Whitmore Reans

19 Riches Street, WV6 0DW

01902 680766

Unlisted

LPA: Wolverhampton

Newhampton

Originally built in 1864, this bustling corner local was much extended on the Riches Street side in 1922 by Atkinsons' Brewery - hence the internal door with an etched window bearing the brewery triple A trademark. Further changes in 1981 saw part of the servery removed, opening up the hall into the front bar area, and closing a door in the middle of the old bar. This area has a terrazzo floor, old fixed seating and possibly old fireplaces but the bar furniture is all modern. At the back, the quiet and elegant smoke room, served by a hatch, is largely intact whilst the former snug, now used for pool, also retains some 1922 features. The crown bowling green behind is served by the separate Pavilion Bar built in 1912 - note the unusual bowls boxes.

Wolverhampton, Whitmore Reans

3 Harrow Street, WV1 4PB

01902 425336

Unlisted

LPA: Wolverhampton

Stile

A late-Victorian back-street pub, with a seemingly unaltered layout, though some changes were apparently made in 1921. On the corner is an excellent plain bar with good chunky counter and old bar back, fixed seating and dado panelling. An L-shaped corridor snakes round the back of the bar and rear left is an old-fashioned smoke room with service to the bar through a door. Across the corridor on the right, a plain room is used for pool. Another small room off the passage has a Victorian fireplace but nothing else. Outside, between the bar and smoke room is a good etched window for the (unused) 'outdoor department'. Unusual L-shaped bowling green behind.

Worcestershire

Birtsmorton

WR13 6AP
01684 833308
Grade II listed
LPA: Malvern Hills

Farmers Arms

Bar fittings were installed, probably for the first time, at this 17th-century pub around 1950, since when little has changed. The small left-hand bar has a plain bar counter and period bar back with glass shelves and old till drawer. Note the dates on the handpumps (1951 and 1952). More 1950s fittings - seating and fireplace - are found in the lower-ceilinged area left of the servery. In the right-hand bar are a chunky bar counter with more date-stamped handpulls and old bar-back shelving, fireplace and settle. Further right, and slightly opened out to a passage, the dining room has more Fifties seating, another old settle, beamed ceiling and half-timbered walls.

The right-hand bar, with 1950s fittings

Bretforton

The Cross, WR11 7JE
01386 831173
Grade II listed
LPA: Wychavon

The Pewter Room

Fleece ★

This legendary pub was owned by the same family for generations, with the last of the line, Miss Lola Taplin, bequeathing it to the National Trust on her death in 1977. Inside the 17th-century building, the three stone-flagged rooms retain Lola's extraordinary assemblage of old furniture and other artefacts. The 'Pewter Room' takes its name from an impressive collection of antique pewterware and has a large settle with doors at the back for storage; note the

'witches circles' near the inglenook fireplace - supposedly efficacious in stopping witches coming down the chimney. The 'Dug Out', down two steps and with a stone fireplace, is the former games room, popular for darts in Lola's time. The 'Brewhouse' is the most striking room with its vast inglenook fireplace and indentations in the wall for feeding in water from the well outside in the days of home brewing. After fire damage in February 2004, the Fleece was carefully restored and reopened in May 2005.

Claines

Claines Lane, WR3 7RN
01905 456649
Unlisted
LPA: Wychavon

The 1930s servery with its counter screens

Mug House

Hidden away in the village churchyard, this three-roomed pub occupies a part-timber-framed 16th-century building. The original plain brick frontage was replaced in the 1980s by false timber-framing with new brick infill but, inside, little has changed since the 1930s. In the quarry-tiled, part-panelled passage, a leaded glass screen with intact sliding hatch for service is a real highlight. The pub was popular with employees of the local Rackstraws furniture works and an apprentice there reputedly made the counter in the smoke

room; this has more old panelling and an inter-war brick fireplace. The small snug on the right, known as 'the kitchen', has a quarry-tiled floor and brick fireplace. At the rear, the lounge is served by a hatch and has a fireplace and baffle from the 1930s but post-war seating.

Clent

Belbroughton Road, Holy Cross,
DY9 9QL
01562 730319
Grade II listed
LPA: Bromsgrove

Bell & Cross ★

A pub for nearly 200 years, the Bell & Cross has grown over time to five separate rooms and, despite the current emphasis on food, a strong sense of the traditional small village pub can still be captured. The central quarry-tiled corridor runs to the rear and the tiny hatch on the left was, no doubt, used for off-sales. Behind is the little public bar with a possibly Victorian counter and bar back plus some old fixed seating; the fireplace is probably inter-war. Right of the entrance, a delightful snug is created by a pair of full-height timber partitions which form the backs to the fixed seating within. Thousands of pub rooms up and down the country would once have resembled this cosy space. Room '6' beyond was apparently once the landlord's living room while Room '4', facing it, was the gentlemen's smoke room. At the back, a further room was created out of a barn in 1998. These last three rooms have been refitted in recent years.

Timber partitions screen off this room at the front of the pub

Defford

A4104 Woodmancote,
WR8 9BW
01386 750234
Grade II listed
LPA: Wychavon
Open Fri and Sun lunchtimes, Weds
and Sat evenings

Cider House ('Monkey House') ★

One of our most unspoilt pubs, the unique Cider House occupies part of a 17th-century thatched, half-timbered building. It has been in the family of landlady Gill Collins for 150 years and is one of four remaining cider-only houses in the country. The main bar is actually outside, viz. the front garden! If the weather disappoints, customers drink in the former bakehouse at the side. Service is through a hatch in a stable door on the left of the cottage with the cider casks stillaged behind in a ground floor 'cellar'. The toilets are outside but the ladies' has the luxury of a roof! The nickname supposedly derives from the tale told by a well-mellowed customer on returning home - he claimed he was covered in cuts and scratches not because of a self-induced collapse into a bramble patch but rather an attack by a tribe of monkeys.

Grimley

Camp Lane, WR2 6LX

01905 640288

Grade II listed

LPA: Malvern Hills

Camp House Inn

Much of what we see dates from around 1936 when the pub was enlarged and a bar added for the first time. During this period, it served a section of the River Severn known as Grimley Lido, popular for sunbathing and swimming. The right-hand bar, slightly extended in the 1970s, has several 1930s features - fireplace, bar counter and handpumps dated 1936 - but modern bar-back. The larger left room also has a Thirties fireplace plus a high-backed settle and service from a hatch cut into the wall. The panelling had to be replaced quite recently after flooding. The entrance on the car park side brings you into a small hall with intact off-sales hatch and split door leading to the staff servery. An uneven tiled-floor passage takes you to the public bar and a small snug, the latter with more flood-replacement panelling but old-looking benches. Plenty of 1930s Crittall windows throughout. Regular floods mean the pub is often closed so best to check ahead before visiting.

Hanley Castle

Church End, WR8 0BL

01684 592686

Grade II listed

LPA: Malvern Hills

The unspoilt public bar

Three Kings ★

This pub has been held by the same family since 1911. The name commemorates not the biblical Three Wise Men but (supposedly) three brothers called King who owned the building many moons ago. The oldest part is on the left where, to the right of the corridor and through a sliding door, you find the gloriously unspoilt public bar. It has a quarry-tiled floor, high-backed settle (doubling as the partition to the corridor), a huge copper-hooded fireplace and a hatch to the servery. Left of the corridor is a little-used smoke room, also with sliding door. The pub's right-hand side houses 'Nell's Lounge', added in 1982 and named after the school-mistress whose house it was. It retains the range from her former kitchen and, at the front, a high-backed settle and an inglenook fireplace with bread oven.

Pensax

On B4202, WR6 6AE
01299 896677
Unlisted

The former parlour

Bell

Although significantly altered around 1980, you can still discern what a true period piece this pub, built in 1883, had been till then. On the left of the red-tiled entrance passage is a three-bay screen, with the lower window of the middle bay open. It was through here that beer used to be served from now-removed handpumps. Behind the screen is a tiny room with wooden floor and a tiled and wood-surround fireplace, above which is a delicate mantelpiece including bevelled mirror sections. This room formerly operated as a parlour for selected customers - others having to drink in the passageway.

The front-right room was used only at busy times whilst, through sliding doors, was a rarely-opened darts/dominoes room. These two rooms were joined up in the alterations and now form the main bar - the bar counter and back were added at this time, as was the small bar counter in the hall. The dining room on the left was formed out of former private rooms.

Stoke Works

Shaw Lane, B60 4BH
01527 861291
Unlisted
LPA: Bromsgrove

Bowling Green

Originally two cottages, this became a pub in 1892 and retains two small front rooms and a rear main bar overlooking an active bowling green. The front left room, created by a curved partition wall, is especially fine with its ancient door, red tiled floor and unusual curved bar counter with small windows above. The fixed seating is old but re-covered and there are old wall cupboards and modest baffles by the door. The front-right-hand snug is served from a small hatch/bar and also has venerable fixed seating. The main lounge bar has been extended but probably many years ago as the panelling and bench seating looks old, though other fittings are modern. Attractive stained glass in the inner door.

Worcester
4 Bull Ring, St Johns, WR2 5AD
01905 421086
Unlisted
LPA: Worcester

Bush ★

A pub built in 1879 which contains two old rooms and some fine fittings. The public bar was once divided into three as evidenced by scars on the counter; it has a couple of bell-pushes and original seating. The star feature, though, is the wonderfully ornate L-shaped bar back, with prominent pediment, twisted columns, mosaic-style

mirrors and a clock which helpfully names the bar fitters, Yates & Greenways of Birmingham. The counter itself has well-crafted fielded panelling. On the left, a now-closed tiled corridor has an off-sales hatch to the servery. A curiosity is that there was formerly a second outlet for take-home supplies - the 'outdoor department' with service through another hatch. The side door and rear corridor lead to a small smoke room with fixed seating and bell-pushes.

The Bush has a servery with a very fine bar back

Worcester
31 Friar Street, WR1 2NA
01905 724006
Grade II listed
LPA: Worcester

Cardinal's Hat

Built originally around 1760, the interior of this pub exemplifies the 'Olde Englishe' style popular between the wars. A passage runs from the front door to the back and has a dado of old panelling. The best of the three small rooms is the rear left bar (numbered 6) whose walls are fully covered in Tudor-style panelling with a stone fireplace to match. Fixed benches line the walls, with bell-pushes above, an intact hatch accesses the back of the servery and the top section of the outside windows sports some colourful glasswork. Front right, a

small snug has imitation half-timbering and lots of leaded window glass but no old fittings and an unused outside door. The same half-timbering appears in the main bar, front left, alongside a stone chimney-piece with a four-centred arch and plaster cardinal's hat above. The old-looking counter dates from a sensitive refurbishment by Banks's in 1996. The toilets retain their tiled walls from the 1930s.

This rear room has fine inter-war Tudor-style panelling and a fireplace

Worcester

Worcester
6 Angel Street, WR1 3QT
01905 21395
Grade II listed
LPA: Worcester

Cricketers

Although the ground-floor layout of this old inn has been compromised, much remains from a quality 1950s refit. In the main bar, panelling on the left-hand walls is in a distinctive 1950s style while the semi-island bar counter and brick fireplace are also redolent of the era. On the right a smaller room/area has a different style of panelling, another period fireplace and fixed seating likely to be of the same date. A baronial-style function room upstairs has more dado panelling in the same style (but painted over) plus some pargetting on the walls depicting heraldic devices, such as roses and lions.

The quality 1950s refit at the Cricketers

Worcester
2 Friar Street, WR1 2LZ
01905 616378
Grade II listed
LPA: Worcester

Closes 7pm Tuesday
& Sunday

Eagle Vaults

The spectacular glazed tile frontage here dates from around 1890 but the building itself is about 150 years older. In the lobby are a colourfully-tiled dado and a mosaic floor running to the back of the pub. There were once walls either side of the passage but changes took place in 1983, hence the wide gap in the left-hand wall. The bare-boarded bar on the right retains its fixed seating, Victorian counter and fine bar back with gilded glass panels and clock on top but the etched windows are replacements. When the wall was taken out, the left-hand curved section of the counter was added and by and large carefully matches the original part. In the smoke room is more old fixed seating in bays, with panels above and bell-pushes all around. The fire surround, with bevelled mirrors in the mantlepiece above, is original as are two splendid etched and frosted windows incorporating an eagle. A function room upstairs has no old fittings.

The servery,
c.1890

Worcester

6 The Butts, WR1 3PA

01905 729290

Grade II listed

LPA: Worcester

Closed Sundays

The public bar and its
fittings of 1901

Paul Pry ★

This wedge-shaped building of 1901 is the work of architect
Frederick Hughes. Beyond the vestibule, through decorative double
doors, is the glorious entrance hall with terrazzo floor and wonderful
multi-coloured wall-to-ceiling tiling. The right-hand side is a
mahogany partition which forms the bar-back fitting and has leaded
panels along the top. An inner door on the far right accesses the old
off-sales with two-part sliding hatch. Nearer the entrance, the door
with a 'Bar' etched panel leads to a virtually intact room with

mahogany bar counter and an elaborate
mirrored and columned bar back, which
has a clock in its pedimented centrepiece
plus cupboard and balustrade. Other fine
features are the Victorian fireplace,
panelled dado, original (but
re-upholstered) benches, Lincrusta
moulded ceiling and, beneath the carpet,
a terrazzo floor. Three of the etched
windows survive. The former smoke
room on the left still has its old fireplace,
Lincrusta frieze and embossed ceiling
but other fittings have been modernised.
A second entrance, in Infirmary Walk,
was closed some years ago to create a
ladies' toilet.

Worcester, Ronkswood

Lichfield Avenue, WR5 1PE

01905 863054

Unlisted

LPA: Worcester

The public bar, 1958

Punch Bowl ★

A true rarity - a post-war pub which has barely altered since opening
(1958 in this case). It serves the local housing estate and is located on
a circular site in the middle of the estate with a church in the centre
and shops round the perimeter. The smallish public bar faces the
circle and has fixed seating, quarry-tiled flooring, brick fireplace,
counter and bar back, all of simple, straightforward design. The

unusual projection on the right was
evidently for darts-playing and the fixed
seat was for players and spectators. To the
rear right is a small pool room then, at the
back, a large function room, extended to
accommodate a skittle alley. Finally, on
the left, are a small smoke room and a
former off-sales, now converted into an
office. The plain fittings throughout
reflect the austerity and desire for simple
clean lines at the end of the 1950s.

Closed Pubs

CAMRA surveys reveal that, at any one time, around 2,000 UK pubs are 'in limbo' – closed for the time being but not necessarily gone for ever. Needless to say, a number of Midlands pubs with important historic interiors fall into this category. We are hopeful that some at least will return to active service under new owners who will appreciate the heritage value of their assets. For others, the outlook is more gloomy, especially as most of them are in areas of towns and cities which are run down or where local custom has moved away.

The following pubs would have been main entries in this guide had they currently been open:

DERBYSHIRE

Somercotes
Leabrooks Road, DE55 4HB
Unlisted
LPA: Amber Valley

Horse & Jockey

A brick-built, late Victorian pub, refitted around 1954 by Home Brewery, and hardly altered since. The interior abounds with period fittings such as ceramic fireplaces, leatherette-padded bench seating and a sloping bar counter with Formica top. Currently up for sale as a pub or alternative use.

WARWICKSHIRE

Coventry
Burnaby Road, CV6 4BU
Listed: Grade II listed
LPA: Coventry

Pilot

This huge inter-war pub has been much altered but impressive Art Deco features survive in two areas. It has been closed since 2011 but there are now proposals to open a pub/restaurant in part of the building – hopefully in one of the aforementioned areas.

Rugby
Bridget Street, CV21 2BG
Unlisted
LPA: Rugby

Engine

Four rooms and some fine etched windows endure in this Victorian back street local, as does a splendid bar back sporting a series of decorative etched panels and visible in the first two rooms. Currently boarded up and for sale as a pub or alternative use.

WEST MIDLANDS

Birmingham, Digbeth
12 Banbury Street, B5 5RH
Unlisted
LPA: Birmingham

Eagle & Tun

One of many tile and terracotta pubs designed around 1900 by James & Lister Lea. Despite much opening up, the original layout is readily discernible and some excellent tiling and bar furniture is still there to be enjoyed. Its proximity to the forthcoming HS2 terminus may assist a comeback.

Birmingham, Handsworth
270 Soho Road, B21 9LK
Grade II* listed
LPA: Birmingham

Red Lion

This fabulous pub of 1901 is now seriously at risk. Behind the flamboyant terracotta facade is a superb multi-roomed interior with a wonderful display of Minton tiling, including a series of tiled paintings in the corridor and a lavish staircase/hall. The narrow public bar has a particularly ornate bar back.

Birmingham, Smethwick
Shireland Road, B66 4RQ
Grade II* listed
LPA: Sandwell

Waterloo

A flagship pub-hotel of 1907 for the nearby Mitchells & Butlers Brewery. The Grill Room in the basement is truly spectacular with its all-over tiling but much fine tiling can be found elsewhere in the building. New owners seem to have good intentions but real progress on restoration has been painfully slow.

Dudley
74 Stafford Street, DY1 1RT
Grade II listed
LPA: Dudley

Shakespeare

Hundreds of Black Country pubs would once have resembled this simply-appointed, three-room drinkers' establishment. Its listing by English Heritage in 1999 was seen as a breakthrough in recognising the rarity and importance of such small, basic pubs. However, its prospects are not good and a future as a restaurant is sadly likely.

50 More To Try

The pubs listed below are classified by CAMRA as having interiors which are 'of some regional historic importance'. In other words, they do not match up to the pretty exacting criteria for a main entry but, nevertheless, retain a fair degree of heritage interest – be it a largely intact layout, or some cherishable fixtures or fittings, or a particular room worthy of note. You can find more details about all these pubs at www.heritagepubs.co.uk, where the drop-down menus allow easy searching by county, place and/or pub name.

DERBYSHIRE

Rose & Crown, Boylestone, New Road, DE6 5AA. A four-room pub with a fine snug with quarry-tiled floor, high-backed settle and panelled walls.

Exeter Arms, Derby, Exeter Place, DE1 2EU. The snug is an interesting remnant, although somewhat altered.

Exeter Arms, Derby

White Hart, Duffield, 36 Town Street, DE56 4GD. A pub to visit for the rear left room, largely unchanged since the rebuilding in 1937.

Devonshire Arms, Hartington, Market Place, SK17 0AL. A good deal of old fittings survive, chiefly in the narrow bar on the right.

Colville Arms, Lullington, Main Street, DE12 8EG. High-backed settles and service via two hatches on the left mark this out as a traditional village pub.

Peacock, Rowsley, Bakewell Road, DE4 2EB. Public bar with distinct areas, one with a superb tiled panel with a peacock, another with a fine bar counter.

Hope & Anchor, Wirksworth, Chesterfield Road, DE4 4ET. Much work remains from a 1930s rebuild.

HEREFORDSHIRE

Green Dragon, Bishops Frome, WR6 5BP. Multi-roomed 17th-century inn whose fittings are partly very old, partly 1960s and partly more recent.

Brewery Inn, Ledbury

Brewery Inn, Ledbury, Bye Street, HR8 2AG. Notable for its snug with quarter-circle bar counter, old dado panelling and benches all round.

Chequers, Leominster, Etnam Street, HR6 8AE. Characterful coaching inn though most of the fixtures and fittings are of no great age.

Carpenters Arms, Walterstone, HR2 0DX. The small, flagstoned bar has always been the only public room here.

LEICESTERSHIRE & RUTLAND

Queens Head, Barwell, 80 High Street, LE9 8DR. Three small rooms survive, although now dwarfed by the massive rear extension.

Greyhound, Hinckley, 9 New Buildings, LE10 1HN. Three rooms off a tiled corridor: the rear bar has old dado panelling, benches and a counter.

Richard III, Leicester

Red Lion, Kegworth, 24 High Street, DE74 2DA. A four-room pub with many old fittings, including etched glass naming some of the rooms.

Ale Wagon, Leicester, 27 Rutland Street, LE1 1RE. A town-centre pub with various features remaining from the rebuilding in 1931, although the main bar counter was installed in 1978.

Black Horse, Leicester, 1 Foxon Street, LE3 5LT. Much of the inter-war refurbishment can still be made out despite later changes.

Richard III, Leicester, 70 Highcross Street, LE1 4NN. Although modernised downstairs, the first floor has the rare arrangement of a counterless bar back and two handpumps serving the function room.

Tap & Mallet, Loughborough, 36 Nottingham Road, LE11 1EU. A Victorian pub much expanded in the inter-war period but with an extensive *c*.1960 refurbishment.

White Hart, Measham, Bosworth Road, DE12 7LG. A four-room terraced pub with some old features, although much refitted *c*.1970.

LINCOLNSHIRE

Nottingham House, Cleethorpes

Nottingham House, Cleethorpes, 5-7 Seaview Street, DN35 8EU. Three-room sea-front pub, with inter-war features (at rear), remodelling *c*.1950, and finally a Tetley refurbishment of the 1980s.

Strugglers, Lincoln, Westgate, LN1 3BG. Largely unspoilt small snug, although otherwise modernised.

Old Whyte Swanne, Louth, Eastgate, LN11 9NP. Good-quality bench seating in the rear lounge in an originally mid 17th-century building.

Three Horseshoes, Scotton, 10 Westgate, DN21 3QX. Of interest for the room that was the centre of the original beerhouse with its perforated bentwood seating.

NORTHAMPTONSHIRE

Dun Cow, Daventry

Dun Cow, Daventry, Brook Street, NN11 5NH. A former coaching inn with early 20th-century public bar fittings. Galleried dining room.

Racehorse, Northampton, 15 Abingdon Square, NN1 4AE. Quite a number of the fittings from this 1930s pub survive.

Locomotive, Wellingborough, 111 Finedon Road, NN8 4AL. Formerly a

Quaker-owned house, this became a pub in 1902 from when parts of the counter and bar back survive.

NOTTINGHAMSHIRE

Royal Oak, Collingham, 44 High Street, NG23 7LB. Much survives from a post-war refurbishment, such as the simple tap room.

Royal Oak, Newark, 17 Castle Gate, NG24 1AZ. Retains a good deal of old fittings from the 1930s to 1960s.

Bell, Nottingham, 18 Angel Row, NG1 6HL. The main historic interest is 1928 refit of the two upper panelled rooms.

Mill, Nottingham, Bagnall Road, Basford, NG6 0JY. Although quite plain, this pub is little altered since a refit of 1964 for Home Brewery.

Old Pear Tree, Nottingham, Bulwell Lane, NG6 0BT. Despite refurbishing in 1986, much of character remains, including four small snugs.

Plough, Nottingham, 17 Peter Street, Radford. Some good survivals from the 1920s Nottingham Brewery tap – glazed screen for former off-sales, terrazzo floor etc.

Swan, Newport

SHROPSHIRE

Swan, Newport, Lower Bar, TF10 7BQ. The tiny snug is by far the best area and has very old, attractively patterned half-height-panelling.

Wheatsheaf, Shifnal, Broadway, TF11 8BB. Much opened out but with an old screened bar in the left-hand room and a distinctive 1930s fireplace in the public bar.

Coach & Horses, Shrewsbury, Swan Hill, SY1 1NP. An old counter in the public bar and an interesting snug whose partition walls are tricky to date.

Staff of Life, Stoke-on-Trent

STAFFORDSHIRE

Albion, Stoke-on-Trent, Hanley, Old Hall Street, ST1 1QT. A once-grand interior, now opened out, but tiling, a panelled snug and a fine bar counter survive.

Crown Hotel, Stoke-on-Trent, Longton, Times Square, ST3 1HD. Fabulous full-height Minton tiling and a terrazzo floor in the front entrance.

Staff of Life, Stoke-on-Trent, Stoke, Hill Street, ST4 1NL. Worth a look for the excellent tiled floors in the passage and (now conjoined) snugs.

Vine, Tutbury, Ludgate Street, DE13 9NG. Although much changed over the years, retains some Victorian and inter-war features.

Vaults, Uttoxeter, Market Place, ST14 8HP. Heritage interest here derives from the unusual layout – three rooms front to back – and the unaltered rear room.

WARWICKSHIRE

Victoria, Rugby

Victoria, Rugby, Lower Hillmorton Road, CV21 3ST. Victorian bar back and splendid etched Mitchells & Butlers windows in the public bar.

White Swan, Stratford-on-Avon, Rother Street, CV37 6NH. A fine old hotel, much altered, but with some historic features in the Oak Room, especially the mid-16th-century wall-painting.

WEST MIDLANDS

Town Wall Tavern, Coventry

New Inn, Birmingham, Harborne, Vivian Road, B17 0DJ. The superb bar back in the main bar is the stand-out feature here, despite its grandeur being reduced by recent changes.

Hen & Chickens, Birmingham, Hockley, Constitution Hill, B19 3LE. Surviving Victorian features include leaded windows, some glass-work and the chunky bar counter.

Cricketers, Birmingham, Small Heath, Little Green Lane, B9 5AX. Inter-war pub with much original panelling, fixed seating and bar furniture (but modern fittings as well).

Sir Robert Peel, Bloxwich, Bull Lane, WS3 2JS. Old curved bar counter, decent bar back and bench seating in the public bar.

Town Wall Tavern, Coventry, Bond Street, CV1 4AH. The must-see here is the 'Donkey Box', one of the country's smallest snugs, just six feet square.

Waggon & Horses, Halesowen, Stourbridge Road, B63 3TU. Victorian bar back with etched mirrored panels in the sloping public bar and old seating in both rooms.

Unicorn, Wollaston, Bridgnorth Road, DY8 3NX. The farmhouse-style back room has rustic benches, a hatch to the servery and a fine stained glass window.

WORCESTERSHIRE

Rose & Crown, Feckenham

Rose & Crown, Feckenham, High Street, B96 6HS. Retains some fittings from a 1930s refurbishment though other features date from the 1960s.

The Selection Criteria for CAMRA's Inventories

What really matters about a pub is its interior. CAMRA's inventories of historic pub interiors focus entirely on the **internal physical fabric** of pubs and what is **authentically old** inside them. In this context a pub's external architecture, fine though it may be, is a side issue.

National or regional significance?

The pubs that qualify for the National Inventory of Historic Pub Interiors (NI) must have outstanding attributes - either a high degree of internal intactness or, where there has been alteration, some truly exceptional features or rooms. Outstanding bars and pub-type rooms in other kinds of establishment, such as hotel bars, theatre bars or railway buffets, are also embraced. Rather less is expected of candidates for a regional inventory of historic pub interiors (RI), although they must retain a significant amount of genuine historic features and/or a good sense of their historic layout. Most pubs included on an RI will have some combination of both.

Age

The main focus of CAMRA's inventories is on pre-1939 interiors – fabric that is much as it was before the Second World War – but some later interiors that have survived unaltered, especially from before the mid-1960s (when the modern mania for of pub refitting and opening-out began in earnest) are now rare and have to be seriously considered too. There is, however, a need for more research to develop appropriate criteria for post-war pubs, and CAMRA is actively pursuing this, with help from York University and in parallel with current work being done by English Heritage. Meanwhile, CAMRA is careful to restrict its present selections to clear cases that have special merit (exceptional merit, in the case of the NI). Interiors later than 1970 do not qualify at all for the NI.

Historic pub fittings, features and plan-form

The emphasis is on items that reflect the premises' historic function **as a pub**, rather than inherited from some other (usually domestic) use of the building, although the line is not always easy to draw. Items of specific interest include such things as fixed settles or bench seating, bar-fittings (counter, bar back), screen partitioning, bell-pushes, dispense equipment and original toilets as well as fittings and décor purpose-designed for pubs (most famously by the Victorians and Edwardians, in decorative glass, joinery, plaster and ceramic work). If features like these survive in abundance, with little lost, the pub is a clear candidate for the NI.

The survival of historic layout is also a crucial factor in assessing NI candidates, but regional inventory candidates too should retain sufficient for their original internal planning to be appreciated and understood. Where a pub has undergone modern extension, as so many have, this need not count against it providing the work has been sensitively done (preferably kept physically separate) and does not seriously compromise its 'historic core'.

The bottom line?

If all that's left is a couple of fixed benches and a bit of matchboard panelling in a largely opened-up pub, inclusion will not be justified as these are commonplace and can be found in large numbers. Many pub interiors too still have a few old features like etched glass or tilework which are irreplaceable and a joy to behold, but CAMRA has been cautious about developing plans for a nationally-led campaign to identify and catalogue them - the hope being that the inspiration for compiling such 'local inventories' will take off at the local level itself. Starting in 2014, however, CAMRA has embarked on two 'pilots', both in Yorkshire (in Barnsley and Sheffield) to serve as exemplars and to give a positive impetus to the whole process.

Factual evidence and informed judgement

CAMRA's inventories set great store by including only what is genuinely old. This ought to be a matter of objective, provable fact and certainly the selections for the Yorkshire Regional Inventory have been authenticated wherever possible from documentary sources like original plans, building records or other archive material. However, where no such material exists, as is often the case, the truth is not always easy to establish. Oral testimony from licensees and older regulars can be an invaluable help but reliance often has to be placed on experience and informed judgement.

Index

Numbers in **bold** indciate illustrated references.
The pubs in the gazetteer are not indexed as they can be easily found through the county listings and their maps.

Editor's Acknowledgements

This book would have been impossible without the immense contributions from CAMRA colleagues, especially fellow members of the Pub Heritage Group.

I am particularly indebted to Andy Shaw for all his work on the design and layout of the book.

Andy gratefully acknowledges the help he has received from Dale Tomlinson, designer of the previous books in this series and on whose templates the design of this book is closely based.

Producing these guides involves a vast amount of survey work; for every pub which gains an entry, several more will have been inspected and found wanting.

Mick Slaughter has carried out a huge number of these surveys and then written them up in detail, providing me with much raw material; he also chauffeured me on several West Midlands surveying trips.

On top of that, Mick is the source of most of the photographs in the book. Nearly all the other photos come from Geoff Brandwood who, in addition, wrote several of the feature articles and spread his verbal fairy dust over my drafts of the other articles and the pub descriptions.

Many initial drafts of the East Midlands pub descriptions were the work of Julian Tubbs and he and Steve Peck did much surveying in that area.

The previous book in this series, *Yorkshire's Real Heritage Pubs*, has been an inspiration as well as an impossible act to follow, so I owe great thanks to its editor, Dave Gamston who also provided invaluable advice on the necessary task of consulting local planning authorities and others.

Final thanks go to the numerous CAMRA members in the Midlands who have suggested pubs for inclusion and provided information about them.

Glossary

Acroterion: (plural, acroteria) a term from classical architecture for an ornament sitting on a flat base such as a pediment.

Ale: originally a fermented malt liquor, made without the use of hops. The term has been effectively interchangeable with 'beer' for at least 200 years.

Art Deco: a fashionable style between the two world wars in Europe and America. It relied on geometrical patterns and sleek lines. The name comes from the Exposition de Art-Décorifs in Paris in 1924-5 which greatly enhanced its popularity.

Art Nouveau: a style relying on flowing lines and sinuous forms, and often based on nature and the human figure. It was popular from about 1890 until 1914, but more in Europe than the UK.

Bar back: the shelving etc. at the rear of the servery, sometimes very ornately treated, for example, with mirrors. In Scotland and Northern Ireland known as a gantry.

Barrel: although widely used as a term for any size of cask, the term applies, strictly speaking, to a vessel containing 36 gallons. It used to be the standard size for beer casks until the mid-20th century. Nowadays the standard cask contains 9 gallons and is properly termed a firkin.

Beerhouse: a place where beer only (not wine or spirits) was sold in former times.

Bottle and jug: see jug and bottle.

Brewers' Tudor: a style, especially popular between the two world wars, drawing nostalgically upon the half-timbered architecture of the Tudor period. Within pubs it was often associated with fully panelled rooms.

Brewers Tudor - Norman Arms, Derby

Brewery tap: a brewery's nearest tied retail outlet.

Cooper: someone who makes wooden casks bound by metal hoops.

Dado: the lower part of a wall, usually wood-panelled, below a rail and above a skirting board.

Drinking lobby/corridor: an area for almost exclusively stand-up drinking, and popular in the north of England. The lobby is very often an expanded corridor area with a bar counter: in corridors there is a hatch to the servery.

Fielded panelling: wooden panels with a raised or sunken square or rectangular central section.

Fielded panelling - Cardinal's Hat, Worcester

Formica: a laminate product, very popular in the 1950s/1960s, for topping counters and other surfaces needing to be kept clean.

Improved public houses: inter-war ones built with the aim of making the pub respectable. They tended to be large, had a wide range of facilities, and sought to attract a better class of customer.

Inglenook: a recess adjoining a fireplace.

Rose & Crown, Feckingham

Inn: premises offering drink, food and accommodation for travellers in earlier centuries. More recently the term has been loosely used by any kind of pub establishment (likewise tavern, q.v.).

Jug and bottle: a space in a pub, usually with a separate entrance from the street, where alcoholic drinks could be purchased for consumption off the premises.

Leatherette: an artificial leather product, made by covering a fabric base with plastic.

Lounge: a better-quality pub room.

Modern: a fairly modest, simplified version of Art Deco (q.v.).

Off-sales: sale of drinks for consumption off the premises (a term sometimes used for the jug and bottle, q.v.).

Pediment: a triangular or sometimes curved gable.

Pubco: a pub-owning company with no brewing interests.

Public house: Literally a house open to the public. The name refers back to much earlier centuries when individuals would open their houses for the sale of drink. In the 19th century 'public house' tended to refer to fully-licensed premises selling all types of intoxicating liquor, as opposed to beerhouses (q.v.) which sold just beer.

Quarry tiles: plain, unglazed floor tiles, usually red and black.

Real ale: a term coined in the early 1970s to describe traditional British beer, which undergoes a secondary fermentation and conditioning in the cask (hence the alternative term 'cask-conditioned).

Roadhouse: a (usually large) inter-war pub beside a main road, often with extensive facilities to attract, for example, families and the new generation of motorists. See also improved public houses.

Saloon: a better-class pub room.

Servery: the area from which drinks are dispensed.

Settle: bench seating, often curved, with a medium to high back.

Smoke room: a better-class pub room.

Snob screens: small, swivelling translucent glazed panels at eye level that provided customers with a degree of privacy.

Snobs screens - Bartons Arms, Birmingham

Snug: a small, intimate drinking space.

Strapwork: stylised representation of leather straps for decorative purposes.

Tap room: a pub room of similar status to the public bar. Despite what the name might suggest, drink was very rarely dispensed within them as they tended to be separate from the servery (see p.87).

Tavern: originally an urban drinking house serving wine and food, mostly to better-off customers. In modern times the term has been adopted by all kinds of pub establishment (likewise tavern, q.v.).

Teetotal: abstaining from all alcoholic drinks.

Temperance: advocacy of drinking little or no alcohol. The earliest campaigners promoted moderation and boycotted only spirits: however, after 1832 increasing numbers became teetotal (q.v.).

Terracotta: (literally fired earth) hard-wearing, unglazed ceramic ware.

Terrazzo: tiny pieces of marble set in concrete, rubbed down and polished.

Tongue and groove: a method of joinery which allows flat boards of wood to be joined into a single flat surface.

Vault(s): for a pub room, an alternative name for a public bar, especially in the north of England.

Vestibule: a hall or passage between an entrance and the main interior of a building.

CAMPAIGN
FOR
REAL ALE

Books for pub & beer lovers

CAMRA Books, the publishing arm of the Campaign for Real Ale, is the leading publisher of books on beer and pubs. Key titles include:

Britain's Best Real Heritage Pubs

Edited by **GEOFF BRANDWOOD**

The definitive guide to over 260 pubs throughout the UK which have interiors of real historic significance – some of them stretching back a century or more – covering a vast spectrum of Britain's architectural and social heritage. Fully-illustrated, the guide's extensive listings are the product of years of surveying and research by CAMRA volunteers dedicated to preserving and protecting our rich pub heritage. With a foreword by Simon Thurley, Chief Executive of English Heritage.

£9.99   ISBN 978 1 85249 304 2

London Heritage Pubs – An inside story

GEOFF BRANDWOOD & JANE JEPHCOTE

The definitive guidebook to London's most unspoilt pubs. Ranging from gloriously rich Victorian extravaganzas to unspoilt community street-corner locals, these pubs not only have interiors of genuine heritage value, they also have fascinating stories to tell. *London Heritage Pubs – An inside story* is a must for anyone interested in visiting and learning about London's magnificent pubs.

£14.99   ISBN 978 1 85249 247 2

Real Heritage Pubs of Wales

Editors **MICHAEL SLAUGHTER & MICK DUNN**

An invaluable guide to over 100 pubs in Wales with historic interiors of real national significance, some of them stretching back a century or more, collected together for the first time in this book. The product of many years of surveying by volunteer members of CAMRA who are dedicated to preserving and protecting the UK's historic pub interiors.

£6.99   ISBN 978 1 85249 275 5